WONDERDADS

THE BEST DAD/CHILD
ACTIVITIES IN PORTLAND

CONTACT WONDERDADS

WonderDads books may be purchased for educational and promotional use. For information, please email us at store@wonderdads.com.

If you are interested in partnership opportunities with WonderDads, please email us at partner@wonderdads.com.

If you are interested in selling WonderDads books and other products in your region, please email us at hiring@wonderdads.com.

For corrections, recommendations on what to include in future versions of the book, updates or any other information, please email us at info@wonderdads.com.

ISBN: 978-1-935153-61-0

First Printing, 2011

10 9 8 7 6 5 4 3 2 1

WONDERDADS PORTLAND
Table of Contents

WELCOME TO WONDERDADS PORTLAND

Like so many other Dads, I love being with my kids, but struggle to find the right work/home balance. We are a part of a generation where Dads play much more of an active role with their kids, yet the professional and financial strains are greater than ever. We hope that the ideas in this book make it a little easier to be inspired to do something that makes you a hero in the eyes of your children.

This part of our children's lives goes by too fast, but the memories from a WonderDads inspired trip, event, meal, or activity last a long time (and will probably be laughed about when they grow up). So plan a Daddy day once a week, make breakfast together every Saturday morning, watch your football team every Sunday, or whatever works for you, and be amazed how long they will remember the memories and how good you will feel about yourself in the process.

Our warmest welcome to WonderDads.

Sincerely,

Jonathan Aspatore, **Founder & Dad**
Charlie (4) and Luke (3)

TOP 10 DAD/CHILD THINGS TO DO IN PORTLAND

THE BEST OF PORTLAND

TOP 5 DAD/CHILD RESTAURANTS IN PORTLAND

TOP 5 DAD/CHILD ACTIVITIES IN PORTLAND

TOP 5 DAD/CHILD OUTDOOR PARKS & LOCATIONS IN PORTLAND

TOP 5 DAD/CHILD THINGS TO DO ON A RAINY DAY

TOP 5 DAD/CHILD THINGS TO DO ON A HOT DAY

TOP 5 DAD/CHILD FULL-DAY ACTIVITIES

TOP 5 DAD/CHILD SPLURGES 💲💲💲

TOP 5 DAD/CHILD MOST MEMORABLE

THE BEST DAD/CHILD
RESTAURANTS

PARKERS WAFFLES & COFFEE

Alberta

1805 NE Alberta St.
Portland, OR 97211
(503) 780-5363 | www.parkerswaffes.com

Waffle window version of the downtown food cart. Build your own waffles with unlimited toppings for five bucks! Indulge your kid's desire for crazy combos. Whether sweet or savory, Parker's Waffles hits the spot!

PODNAH'S BBQ

Alberta

1469 NE Prescott St.
Portland, OR 97211
(503) 281-3700 | www.podnahspit.com

Enjoy hibachi–style cuisine, where chefs wow you with their knife skills as they cook vegetables, meat, and noodles right at your table.

TIN SHED GARDEN CAFÉ

Alberta

1438 NE Alberta St.
Portland, OR 97211
(503) 288-6966 | www.tinshedgardencafe.com

The Tin Shed offers whimsically–named dishes such as Fungus Among Us, Peter Piper Picked a Pesto, and the Gladly Pay You Tuesday Burger, along with a commitment to preparing and serving sustainable food that satisfies both stomach and soul. Standouts include the potato cakes and house-baked sweet potato French toast. The Shed's kids menu features simple yet tasty dishes like Olly Olly Oatmeal which is sweetened with banana, raisins, and brown sugar and Cinnamon Swirl French Toast. Dine on the dog-friendly patio.

VITA CAFÉ

Alberta

3023 NE Alberta St.
Portland, OR 97211
(503) 335-8233 | www.vita-café.com

Tops for the Vegetarian/Vegan lifestyle. Organic, local, sustainable, and kid friendly.

BIJOU CAFÉ

Downtown

132 SW 3rd Ave.
Portland, OR 97204
(503) 222-3187

Fresh, organic ingredients, some locally sourced and some selectively imported, form the foundation for simple, healthy, flavorful food. There are more than enough choices on the menu to keep daddy and the troops content.

14

BLUEPLATE LUNCH COUNTER   Downtown

308 SW Washington St.
Portland, OR 97204
(503) 295-2583 | www.eatatblueplate.com

Featured on the Food Network's *Diners, Drive Ins, and Dives*, Blue Plate is every dad's and kid's dream come true. Classic American comfort food that appears to exist in a time warp. Perfectly executed meatloaf, burgers, and grilled cheese, plus retro treats like ice cream sodas, root beer floats, and even egg creams make this old school lunch joint really hop!

KENNY AND ZUKE'S   Downtown

1038 SW Stark St.
Portland, OR 97205
(503) 222-DELI (3354) | www.kennyandzukes.com

You'll want to take the whole mishpucha (family) to nosh on the best pastrami in town, hands down. The bagels and lox practically demand a Sunday New York Times to go with them. Plus, Kenny and Zuke's has the only kids menu in town featuring latkes!

MAMA MIA TRATTORIA   Downtown

439 SW 2nd Ave.
Portland, OR 97204
(503) 295-6464 | www.mamamiatrattoria.com

Lisa Schroeder's sister restaurant to Mother's Bistro, the focus here is on Italian comfort food. The Chicken Parm will have you singing "That's Amore," while the kids menu is sure to be a hit with meatball and linguine, mini pizza, chicken fingers, and pasta and butter.

MOTHER'S BISTRO   Downtown

212 SW Stark St. (corner of Second Ave)
Portland, OR 97204
(503) 464-1122 | www.mothersbistro.com

Chef extraordinaire Lisa Schroeder serves up some of the best home cooking this side of your mom's kitchen in a warm inviting space in the heart of downtown Portland. From comfort food such as mac and cheese du jour and the extraordinary meatloaf, to H and H bagels flown in twice weekly from Manhattan and served with homemade gravlax, Mother's Bistro hits that sweet spot in your soul.

RESTAURANTS

PARKERS WAFFLES & COFFEE   Downtown

SW 4th Ave. & SW College St.
Portland, OR 97211
(503) 780-5363 | www.parkerswaffes.com

Part of Portland's burgeoning food cart scene, Parker's Waffles puts an innovative spin on waffles, with fantastic creations such as the Pulled Pork Waffle: smothered in barbecue sauce, wrapped like a burrito, and served with or without coleslaw, it works to great effect, the perfect marriage of sweet and salty. Kids will be partial to the fruit waffle combos such as Peach Pie and Apple Crisp. Be on the lookout for the Fried Chicken Waffle and the Deep Fried Waffle coming soon, as word on the street is that Parker's Waffologists are hard at work in a subterranean waffle laboratory creating the waffles of tomorrow, today!

ROCCO'S PIZZA   Downtown

949 SW Oak St.
Portland, OR 97205
(503) 223-9835 | www.roccospizza.org

A big fat slice of cheesy goodness just a hop, skip, and a jump from Powell's Books, this PDX Pizzeria will put a smile on your kids' faces!

ROCK BOTTOM BREWERY   Downtown

206 SW Morrison St.
Portland, OR 97204
(503) 796-2739 | www.rockbottom.com

Rock solid pub fare with plenty of options for the young ones. Dishes like grilled cheese, buttered noodles, mac and cheese, and Rocky's burger will keep them smiling. For a sweet treat, try the "make your own sundae."

SUPERDOG   Downtown

1033 SW 6th Ave.
Portland, OR 97204
(503) 719-4009 | www.superdogpdx.com

It's a bird, it's a plane, its SuperDog! Try the Portland Original Dog, made with Zenner's double smokie cooked in local microbrewed beer; for a buck more try it Portland Style with grilled peppers, onions, mushrooms, and Swiss cheese.

APIZZA SCHOLLS   Hawthorne/Belmont

4741 SE Hawthorne Blvd
Portland, OR 97215
(503) 233-1286 | www.apizzascholls.com

Anthony Bourdain is a fan and visited Apizza Scholls for the Portland-themed episode of his "No Reservations" television show.

BARLEY MILL PUB
Hawthorne/Belmont

1629 SE Hawthorne Blvd
Portland, OR 97214
(503) 231-1492

With a funky, hippie vibe, kids will "dig" the sixties memorabilia, fun upstairs loft, and delicious burgers. Mellow your munchies with some groovy "Scooby snacks!"

BURGERVILLE
Hawthorne/Belmont

1122 SE Hawthorne Blvd
Portland, OR 97214
(503) 230-0479 | www.burgerville.com

The Pacific Northwest's ubiquitous burger chain keeps McDonalds and the Burger King in check with its superior product and focus on using local ingredients and sustainable practices, from the Tillamook Cheddar on the burgers and the Oregon blackberries and strawberries used in the shakes, the Walla Walla onion rings, not to mention the hormone free beef raised by local ranchers who actually visit the restaurants. How often do you have the opportunity to talk with the people who raised the beef in the burger you are eating at a fast food restaurant? The kid's meals even contain wonderful educational toys like Oregon wildlife-themed coloring books complete with stickers and crayons or little planters with seeds. This is a fast-food meal you can feed to your kids guilt-free!

CHEESE BAR
Hawthorne/Belmont

6031 SE Belmont St.
Portland, OR 97215
(503) 222-6014 | www.cheese-bar.com

An expertly assembled selection of fine cheeses, plus sandwiches, salads, paired with thoughtful beer and wine choices.

CUP AND SAUCER
Hawthorne/Belmont

3566 SE Hawthorne Blvd
Portland, OR 97214
(503) 236-6001 | www.cupandsaucercafe.com

Breakfast, lunch, or dinner, you will love the food and commitment to sustainability.

NICHOLAS RESTAURANT
Hawthorne/Belmont

318 SE Grand Ave.
Portland, OR 97214
(503) 235-5123 | www.nicholasrestaurant.com

A Middle Eastern culinary adventure for dad and the tots. You haven't lived till you've tried Lebanese Pizza. Follow it up with Mango Cheesecake. Yum!

OASIS CAFÉ
Hawthorne/Belmont

3701 SE Hawthorne Blvd
Portland, OR 97214
(503) 231-0901 | www.oasiscafe.com

Kids will love to build their own pizza at this charming Hawthorne pizzeria. Choose from six sauces and more than forty toppings, including walnuts, shrimp, and even wild boar!

PARADOX CAFÉ
Hawthorne/Belmont

3439 SE Belmont St.
Portland, OR 97214
(503) 232-7508 | www.paradoxorganiccafe.com

Lovely Belmont spot with a focus on organic, vegetarian, and vegan food. Try the Phake Philly or the Tempeh Reuben.

PINE STATE BISCUITS
Hawthorne/Belmont

3640 SE Belmont St.
Portland, OR 97214
(503) 236-3346 | www.pinestatebiscuits.com

Did someone say biscuits and gravy? It doesn't get much better than this warm and flaky Portland jewel.

SLAPPY CAKES
Hawthorne/Belmont

4246 SE Belmont St.
Portland, OR 97215
(503) 477-4805 | www.slappycakes.com

Make your own pancakes! Get your kids to work for you by convincing them that cooking for daddy is fun! Tabletop griddles make it all possible at this fun kid-friendly breakfast joint.

THE WAFFLE WINDOW
Hawthorne/Belmont

3610 SE Hawthorne Blvd
Portland, OR 97214
(503) 239-4756

A hit with dads and kids alike. This neighborhood waffle spot sports highly unusual waffle varieties, such as the Ham and Cheese Waffle, the Chocolate Waffle, the Pumpkin Pie Waffle, and the classic Waffle Ice Cream Sandwich.

UTOPIA CAFÉ
Hawthorne/Belmont

3308 SE Belmont St.
Portland, OR 97214
(503) 235-7606

Great spot to start your day. Try a delicious breakfast scramble or some fried cornmeal with syrup.

AUNT TILLIE'S DELI
Hollywood

2000 NE 42nd Ave.
Portland, OR 97213
(503) 281-1834

Plenty of basics like Grilled Cheese, Peanut Butter & Jelly, and bagels for the little ones. Dads, try the Reuben or the B.L.T, and top it off with a local microbrew.

HOLLYWOOD BURGER BAR
Hollywood

4211 NE Sandy Blvd
Portland, OR 97213
(503) 288-8965 | www.hollywoodburgerbar.com

Old school burger joint with some of the best burgers in town. The Triple Thick Milkshakes are reason enough to pay a visit.

POOR RICHARD'S RESTAURANT
Hollywood

3907 NE Broadway St.
Portland, OR 97232
(503) 288-5285 | www.poorrichardstwofer.com

Since 1959, Portland families have been coming to this venerable Hollywood establishment for delicious food. In 1972, Two-Fers (as in two meals for the price of one) were added to the menu, and rapidly became a tradition. Your kids will love the "choose your own topping" burger.

ALAMEDA BREWHOUSE
Irvington/Lloyd District

4765 NE Fremont St.
Portland, OR 97213
(503) 460-9025 | www.alamedabrewhouse.com

Burgers and fries for the small fry, fine Northwestern cuisine and microbrews for Dad! Try the Beer Battered Prawns and Chips or the "Black Bear Stout" Turkey Pot Pie.

ALAMEDA CAFÉ
Irvington/Lloyd District

4641 NE Fremont St.
Portland, OR 97213
(503) 284-5314 | www.thealamedacafe.com

A real local's café. Terrific breakfasts, featuring French toast made with baguette, deep-fried with a cinnamon-sugar cornflake crust.

RESTAURANTS

19

GRILLED CHEESE GRILL
Irvington/Lloyd District

1027 NE Alberta St.
Portland, OR 97211
(503) 206-8959 | www.grilledcheesegrill.com

Finally, a food cart devoted exclusively to that classic kid's favorite, grilled cheese. The grooviest of indoor seating is provided in a converted old school bus! Kids will go for "the kindergartener," a standard grilled cheese on white, while dads can embrace the glory that is "The Cheesus," a cheeseburger with two grilled cheese sandwiches serving as the "bun."

LUCCA
Irvington/Lloyd District

3449 NE 24th Ave.
Portland, OR 97212
(503) 287-7372 | www.luccapdx.com

Lucca's kid's dinner menu rocks! For $6 you get a drink, an entrée, and an ice cream sundae! The cheese pizza is straight to the point, nothin' fancy. Perfect for dad, too. Try the braised rabbit with carrots and porcini mushrooms. Just don't let the kids know you're eating bunny! Wash it down with a Luccarita.

KEN'S ARTISAN PIZZA
Laurelhurst

304 SE 28th Ave.
Portland, OR 97214
(503) 517-9951 | www.kensartisan.com

Some of Portland's best pizzas are fire-baked at Ken's Artisan Pizza. Inspired by the best pizzas of Italy, Ken's uses local, seasonal ingredients to create simple, delicious masterpieces.

SCREEN DOOR
Laurelhurst

2337 East Burnside St.
Portland, OR 97214
(503) 542-0880 | www.screendoorrestaurant.com

Southern cooking made with local ingredients, including organic meats and produce. Kids will enjoy the Backyard Burger and sides like macaroni and cheese, low-country creamy grits, sweet potato fries, and cornbread.

CALDERA PUBLIC HOUSE
Mt. Tabor

6031 SE Stark St.
Portland, OR 97215
(503) 233-8242 | www.calderapublichouse.com

Housed in a century old structure on the slope of an extinct volcano, this fine establishment serves up some of the best pub grub in town. Soak up the history, the views, and the brews!

ACAPULCO'S SOUTHWEST GOLD
Multnomah Village

7800 SW Capitol Hwy.
Portland, OR 97219
(503) 244-0771

Fun and friendly Mexican food served up with a smile. Mellow, low key atmosphere is perfect for the little ones. Festive piñatas adorn the ceiling and a cheerful staff makes you feel welcome at this friendly neighborhood establishment.

DOWN TO EARTH CAFÉ
Multnomah Village

7828 SW 35th Ave.
Portland, OR 97219
(503) 452-0196 | www.downtoearthcafe.com

Persian cuisine for dad and pub fare for the kids. Located in historic Multnomah Village, the warm and friendly staff will make you feel right at home.

FAT CITY CAFÉ
Multnomah Village

7820 SW Capitol Hwy.
Portland, OR 97219
(503) 245-5457

A diner with all the right moves for a kid friendly meal; lots of quirky kitsch on the walls, simple familiar food done well, criss–cut fries and a friendly and accommodating staff. Only downside is its popularity; the place is regularly packed.

LUCKY LABRADOR'S PUBLIC HOUSE
Multnomah Village

7675 SW Capitol Hwy.
Portland, OR 97219
(503) 244-2537 | www.luckylab.com

Gourmet pizzas, fresh, salads, and Lucky Labs famous cask-conditioned ales, nitro tap beers and rotating guest taps keep dad refreshed. Try the Dog Breath pizza, a dastardly combination of spicy sauce, roasted garlic, fresh minced garlic, red onion, and black olive or maybe the Hot Diggity Dog, smothered in spicy sauce, pepperoni, Italian sausage, black olive, and mushroom.

RESTAURANTS

21

MARCO'S CAFÉ AND ESPRESSO BAR

Multnomah Village

Corner of SW 35th and Multnomah Blvd.
Portland, OR 97219
(503) 245-0199 | www.marcoscafe.com

Great food and fair trade espresso in a fun and festive atmosphere. Dads, try the Tarragon Walnut Chicken Salad on hazelnut bread. Kids can choose from classic entrees like Peanut Butter and Jelly or Mac and Cheese from the terrific kids menu.

FIRE ON THE MOUNTAIN

North Portland

4225 N Interstate Ave.
Portland, OR 97227
(503) 280-WING (9464) | www.portlandwings.com

Wings done to perfection plus wonderful sandwiches and even vegan choices. Try the G.W. Carver Peanut Sandwich, with grilled chicken breast smothered in spicy peanut sauce, Asian slaw, and wasabi mayo, or the Portabello Mushroom Sandwich, with onions, tomato, and garlic mayo. It's just too much goodness for one place!

LOVELY'S FIFTY-FIFTY

North Portland

4039 N Mississippi St. Ste. 101
Portland, OR 97227
(503) 281-4060 | www.lovelyfiftyfifty.com

Perfect pizza, soups, salads, and ice cream, what more do you need? How about wild ice cream flavors like malted milk ball, salted caramel, and burnt honey boysenberry?

MCMENAMINS ST. JOHNS THEATER AND PUB

North Portland

8203 N Ivanhoe St.
Portland, OR 97203
(503) 283-8520 | www.mcmenamins.com

Originally an exhibit hall for Portland's Lewis and Clark Exposition, this 1905 structure now features the familiar McMenamin's mix of burgers, beer, and flicks. Don't worry, Dads are welcome at the "Mommy Matinees."

AMERICAN DREAM PIZZA

Northeast Portland

4620 NE Glisan St.
Portland, OR 97213
(503) 230-0699 | www.americandreampizzapdx.com

Choose from over forty toppings for your pizza or salad! Try the Indigos Blue Plate Special for the little ones.

CADILLAC CAFÉ   Northeast Portland

1801 NE Broadway St.
Portland, OR 97232
(503) 287-4750

One of Portland's best bets for breakfast. Try the Tex-Mex Breakfast Burrito or the Cajun' Catfish with eggs and toast. For the kid who can't make up his or her mind, order the Bunkhouse Vittles sampler platter which is a feast of eggs, potatoes, chicken apple sausage, and hazelnut French custard toast.

FRANKS A LOT (DOG HOUSE)   Northeast Portland

2845 E Burnside St.
Portland, OR 97214
(503) 239-3647

Franks A Lot serves up so many varieties of dogs, they win "best in show" for frankfurters!

HORN OF AFRICA   Northeast Portland

5237 NE MLK Jr. Blvd.
Portland, OR 97211
(503) 331-9844 | www.hornofafrica.net

If your kids are up for a culinary adventure, then this is it! Not the same old burgers and fries, Horn of Africa presents East African and Middle Eastern cuisines that are soul-satisfyingly delicious. Check out their booth at the Portland Saturday Market, too! Try the Sambusa, a triangular pastry filled with beef, chicken, or organic lentils, and seasoned with East African Herbs and spices. For dessert, sample house treats such as Mutabaq, which are African Donuts. Mmmm...Mutabaq.

KENNEDY SCHOOL   Northeast Portland

5736 NE 33rd Ave.
Portland, OR 97211
(503) 249-3983| www.mcmenamins.com/427-kennedy-school-home

Go back to school with your kids at this former elementary school converted into a hotel and restaurant. Don't tell the teacher about the Brewery in the back!

MILO'S CITY CAFÉ   Northeast Portland

1325 NE Broadway
Portland, OR 97232
503.288.6456 | www.miloscitycafe.com

Good ol' pub grub your kids will flip for. The Milo Burger piled high with cheese, fresh herb mayo, and caramelized onions is a feast for dad, and the Peanut Butter and Jelly Stuffed French Toast is a taste treat for the kids. Plus, breakfast is served until 2:30 pm.

RESTAURANTS

23

OLD WIVES' TALES
Northeast Portland

1300 E Burnside
Portland, OR 97214
(503) 238-0470 | www.oldwivestalesrestaurant.com

This Eastside restaurant truly understands kids and their needs. The Children's Playroom for toddlers to ten-year-olds will allow dad to enjoy the multi-ethnic panoply of menu options while the kids have fun. Be sure not to leave without trying the exemplary Hungarian Mushroom Soup.

RUSSELL STREET BAR-B-QUE
Northeast Portland

325 NE Russell St.
Portland, OR 97212
(503) 528-8224 | www.russellstreetbbq.com

Demonstrate your gustatory mettle to your progeny by ordering the mighty "meatapalooza," featuring your choice of three meats, choice of breads, and two sides. Best bets include the smoked beef brisket, the house-smoked pulled pork, and the chopped smoked turkey. Don't forget the Slaw and the Mess O' Greens. Kids will dig into the Creamy Goodness Macaroni and Cheese and the delectable Candied Yams. For a treat try the homemade Banana Pudding, which is layered with Nilla wafers, banana slices, and topped with whipped cream.

SALTY'S ON THE COLUMBIA RIVER SEAFOOD GRILL
Northeast Portland

3839 NE Marine Dr.
Portland, OR 97211
(503) 288-4444 | www.saltys.com

If you're an old salt, then you'll want to take your little sea monkeys to Salty's for their award winning seafood. Savor the marine riches of the Pacific Northwest and beyond on the banks of the Columbia River. Nice kid's menu with fish and chips, grilled cheese, Shirley Temple, Roy Rogers, and more.

SIGNAL STATION PIZZA
Northeast Portland

8302 N Lombard
Portland, OR 97203
(503) 286-2257 | www.signalstationpizza.com

Located in a historic gas station serving hot pizza made with organic flour, fresh salads, and more, this St. John's pizza joint is where it's at!

SUB SHOP #19
Northeast Portland

4331 NE Killingsworth St.
Portland, OR 97218
(503) 281-2609

Tasty sandwiches and rice bowls. A quick and easy lunch spot.

BESAW'S
Northwest

2301 NW Savier St.
Portland, OR 97210
(503) 228-2619 | www.besaws.com

Since 1903, Besaw's has been serving wholesome, delicious fare to Portlanders. Try this neighborhood spot for breakfast, lunch, or dinner. The Wild Salmon Scramble is a Pacific Northwest treat.

ELEPHANTS DELICATESSEN
Northwest

115 NW 22nd Ave.
Portland, OR 97210
(503) 299-6304 | www.elephantsdeli.com

One of Portland's most venerable delis. You've got to try the Mama Leone's Chicken Soup and their wood–fired pizzas. Kids will love the tomato–orange soup and grilled cheese sandwich.

ESCAPE FROM NEW YORK PIZZA
Northwest

622 NW 23rd Ave.
Portland, OR 97210
(503) 227-5423

Close your eyes, take that first bite, and you might forget that New York is 3,000 miles away. Thin crust, whole milk mozzarella, and homemade sauce make the perfect pizza trifecta.

KETTLEMAN BAGEL COMPANY
Northwest

2314 NW Lovejoy St.
Portland, OR 97210
(503) 295-2314 | www.kettlemanbagels.com

Finally, a bagel Portlanders can be proud of. Traditional New York style bagel boiled and baked to chewy perfection. Try their superior whitefish, quite possibly the best in Portland, or their Oregon Lox.

KORNBLATT'S DELICATESSEN
Northwest

628 NW 23rd Ave.
Portland, OR 97210
(503) 242-0055

This New York style Jewish deli has been a vital lifeline for East Coast transplants to Portland for many years. Whether you're pining for home à la Joel Fleischman or just hungry for a nosh, you'll be beckoned by the overflowing bucket of pickles on the table and one of the widest selections of smoked fish in town. Best bets are the Matzoh Ball Soup and the Sloppy Joes, which are no "manwiches." Instead they are an authentic re-creation of the Northern New Jersey version of the sandwich, consisting of three thin slices of rye, your choice of deli meat or cheese, coleslaw and Russian dressing. Badda-Bing!

25

ROSE'S RESTAURANT AND BAKERY

Northwest

838 NW 23rd Ave.
Portland, OR 97210
(503) 222-5292 | www.eatatroses.com

Since 1956, Rose's has served up home-cooked deli meals to the people of Portland. You'll love the "New Yorker," hot corned beef topped with cole-slaw and Thousand Island dressing on grilled rye. Your kids will dig Rose's Chicken Tenders or Grilled Cheese.

SKYLINE RESTAURANT

Northwest

1313 NW Skyline Blvd.
Portland, OR 97229
(503) 292-6727

Since 1935, Skyline is "Tops For Hamburgers" in Portland. Real old-fash-ioned ice cream and shakes make this authentic diner a must visit desti-nation for locals and visitors alike.

STEPPING STONE CAFÉ

Northwest

2390 NW Quimby St.
Portland, OR 97210
(503) 222-1132 | www.steppingstonecafe.com

Classic diner food is on tap at Stepping Stone. Stop by for breakfast, lunch or dinner, all the classics are here from Chicken-Fried Steak, Cheese Blintz-es, Reubens, the Big Salad, and Whole Wheat Man-Cakes as featured on the Travel Channel's _Man Versus Food_ show.

TYPHOON! PORTLAND UPTOWN

Northwest

2310 NW Everett St.
Portland, OR 97210
(503) 243-7557 | www.typhoonrestaurants.com

Kid friendly dishes such as Chicken Satay, Pot Stickers, and Pad Thai abound. When in season, Mango Sticky Rice makes a healthy and deli-cious dessert option. Wash it down with an ice cold Singha, Thailand's signature beer or choose from over 150 different types of tea!

ALEXIS RESTAURANT   Old Town/Chinatown

215 W Burnside St.
Portland, OR 97209
(503) 224-8577 | www.alexisfoods.com

Geared toward the more adventurous young eater, this family-oriented Greek eatery specializes in home style Mediterranean delights. Highlights include the Spanikopita, the Moussaka, the Dolmathes, and their home-made "Alexis Bread."

GOLDEN HORSE   Old Town/Chinatown
SEAFOOD RESTAURANT

238 NW 4th Ave.
Portland, OR 97209
(503) 228-1688 | www.thegoldenhorse.info

Generous portions and a family atmosphere make this Chinatown stop a sure bet.

OLD TOWN PIZZA   Old Town/Chinatown

226 NW Davis St.
Portland, OR 97209
(503) 222-9999 | www.oldtownpizza.com

Built above Portland's infamous Shanghai Tunnels, you'll be shanghaied to good taste! Featured on Rachel Ray's Tasty Travels, this old town charmer is even rumored to be haunted. Please don't disturb Nina, the restaurant's ghostly denizen. Choose from 30 pizza toppings and dig into a crispy crust made with sustainable flour. Dishes such as paninis, spaghetti and meatballs, and salads. Plus, Portland microbrews are sure to please the whole crew.

THE HOUSE OF LOUIE   Old Town/Chinatown

331 NW Davis St.
Portland, OR 97209
(503) 228-9898

Dim Sum and more. Kids will like the dragon festooned interior and old school Chinese food. Dads will devour the Ginger Chicken and the Kung Pao.

THE REPUBLIC   Old Town/Chinatown

222 NW 4th Ave.
Portland, OR 97209
(503) 226-4388

Operating in the same location since 1930, step into a page from Portland's yesteryear and soak up the vintage décor and charm of this Chinatown jewel. Classic Cantonese dishes such as Chop Suey, Chow Mein, and Lo Mein are kid friendly and sure to please!

27

VEGETARIAN HOUSE
Old Town/Chinatown

22 NW 4th Ave.
Portland, OR 97209
(503) 274-0160 | www.vegetarianhouse.com

Try the "fish," "chicken," and "shrimp"! All three are plant-based simulations of course, but if you or your children are vegetarian or vegans, this is your Chinese restaurant!

GRAND CENTRAL BAKERY & CAFÉ
Sellwood/Westmoreland

7987 SE 13th Ave.
Portland, OR 97202
(503) 546-3036 | www.grandcentralbakery.com

Incomparable hearth-baked breads compliment the fresh, local, and seasonally available ingredients in Grand Central's masterful sandwiches. Throw in soup or salad, and a pastry, and you've got yourself a feast for a reasonable price. Don't worry, there's Grilled Cheese and PB and J for the kids.

POK POK
Sellwood/Westmoreland

3226 SE Division St.
Portland, OR 97202
(503) 232-1387 | www.pokpokpdx.com

Serving Thai lunch and dinner, you will find unique dishes and desserts that will keep you coming back for more. Children will love the messy goodness of the Coconut Ice Cream Sandwich. Dad will want to sample the Pok Pok Affogato; the blissful union of ice cream and coffee served with a donut....mmm...donuts.

BIPARTISAN CAFÉ
Southeast Portland

7901 SE Stark St.
Portland, OR 97215
(503) 253-1051 | www.bipartisancafe.com

This politically-themed café will bring the people together as never before! Soups, sandwiches, homemade pie, and Stumptown Coffee cross party lines and reach across the aisle with good taste. Live music and book readings too.

BUNK SANDWICHES
Southeast Portland

621 SE Morrison St.
Portland, OR 97214
(503) 477-9515 | www.bunksandwiches.com

Perfectly executed, simple, delicious sandwiches. Standouts include the Grilled Tillamook Cheddar, Meatball Parmigiano Hero, Pork Belly Cubano sandwich and more.

DOUG FIR LOUNGE
Southeast Portland

830 E Burnside St.
Portland, OR 97214
(503) 231-9663 | www.dougfirlounge.com

Rockin' by night, kid-friendly by day. The Lil' Spruce Menu for kids 11 & younger will fit the bill.

FLYING PIE PIZZERIA
Southeast Portland

7804 SE Stark St.
Portland, OR 97215
(503) 254-2016

Featuring pizza, calzones, subs, and pasta, this is the place to fill 'er up after a day at Washington Park.

GRAND CENTRAL RESTAURANT AND BOWLING
Southeast Portland

SE 8th & Morrison St.
Portland, OR 97232
(503) 236-BOWL (2695) | www.thegrandcentralbowl.com

Great place for kids' birthdays or just a night out bowling with dad. Food options include nachos, mac and cheese, and sliders for the kids and dishes like Kung Pao shrimp, chicken carbonara, grilled ahi tuna and more for dad.

LUCKY LABRADOR BREW PUB
Southeast Portland

915 SE Hawthorne Blvd.
Portland, OR 97214
(503) 236-3555 | www.luckylab.com

A great neighborhood hangout for kids, dads, and dogs. Canines are very welcome at the Lab. One of the best local brewpubs, with a focus on cask conditioned ales similar to those served in Britain. These tasty ales are brewed without carbon dioxide, and served at room temperature, as cold can serve to mask the true flavor of the beer. Kids will love the PB and J, the grilled cheese, and the yummy cheese pizza.

MY FATHER'S PLACE
Southeast Portland

523 SE Grand Ave.
Portland, OR 97214
(503) 235-5494 | www.myfathersplace.com

For WonderDads, the name says it all. A great place for breakfast. Try the hot, fluffy pancakes, or choose from over a dozen different toppings and build your own omelet or scramble.

ORIGINAL HOTCAKE HOUSE   Southeast Portland

1002 SE Powell Blvd.
Portland, OR 97202
(503) 236-7402

Old school hotcakes, no frills breakfast, includes giant 3 egg omelettes, waffles and French toast. Big, fluffy stacks of heaven, drowning in a sea of maple and buttery goodness. Great burgers and fries for lunch, smothered in melted cheese and generous toppings. Chase it down with ice-cold thick milkshakes. Dig the vinyl booths and rockin' jukebox, this is a flapjack joint that doesn't need to try to be retro.

SPEEDBOAT COFFEE   Southeast Portland

5115 SE Foster Rd.
Portland, OR 97206
(503) 775-6622 | www.speedboatcoffee.com

Great coffee, awesome playroom, need we say more?

THE OBSERVATORY   Southeast Portland

8115 SE Stark St.
Portland, OR 97215
(503) 445-6284 | www.theobservatorypdx.com

The lunch menu has plenty of options for kids, such as the Burger Burger, six ounces of cascade natural beef with fries, or the yummy Grilled Cheese made with Tillamook cheddar.

WYEAST PIZZA   Southeast Portland

3131 SE 50th Ave.
Portland, OR 97206
(503) 701-5149 | www.wyeastpizza.com

Baked in an 800 degree oven in a converted 1974 RV, Wy'east Pizza has a rustic touch and the perfect blend of mozzarella, tomato sauce, and crispy crust.

ZELL'S AN AMERICAN CAFÉ   Southeast Portland

1300 SE Morrison St.
Portland, OR 97214
(503) 239-0196

Family-friendly neighborhood restaurant specializing in breakfast. Try the smoked wild salmon scramble or the yummy Portland Potatoes.

A SLICE OF NEW YORK   Southwest Portland

7410 SW Oleson Rd.
Portland, OR 97223
(503) 245-1079

Finally, a pizza in Southwest Portland made with Bronx style. Two guys from the Bronx, Pat and Charlie, bring their skills to Oregon. Thin crust, home made sauce, whole milk mozzarella made in New York, all baked to bubbling perfection. Now this is Pizza! Throw in hero sandwiches that are truly heroic; witness the might of the Meatball Parmigiana Hero; toss in some delicious house specialties like Eggplant Parmigiana, Manicotti, and Cannelloni, and you've got an Italian feast fit for a king. Mangia!

ART LARRANCE'S RACCOON   Southwest Portland
LODGE & BREWPUB

7424 SW Beaverton-Hillsdale Hwy.
Portland, OR 97225
(503) 296-0110 | www.raclodge.com

No you won't find Ralph Kramden or Ed Norton here, but you will find great food and some of Portland's best beer brewed on the premises in the Cascade brewery. They specialize in Northwest sour-style beers, such as Frite Galois, a Belgian-style sour ale or Sang Rouge which is aged for as long as thirty months in oak barrels. The kids menu keeps 'em happy with corn dogs, chicken strips, and quesadillas.

BISCUITS CAFÉ   Southwest Portland

460 SW Miller Rd.
Portland, OR 97225
(503) 297-3880 | www.biscuitscafe.com

One of Portland's best bets for breakfast in a city that loves breakfast. Lacking the pretense of some other more upscale establishments, Biscuits gives the people what they want. Prices are very reasonable, service and coffee refills are prompt, the food is great and the portions are generous. Don't miss the sweet potato pancakes! Biscuits is also open for lunch and dinner.

CAFÉ AT THE J   Southwest Portland

6651 SW Capitol Hwy.
Portland, OR 97219
(503) 535-3630 | www.portlandjewishacademy.org

The only kosher dairy restaurant in Portland and certified by Oregon K. The café is open Sunday through Friday. On Tuesday nights the restaurant offers a kosher meat buffet-style dinner, cooked in the catering kitchen.

31

CIDER MILL/ FRYER TUCK CHICKEN

Southwest Portland

6712 SW Capitol Hwy.
Portland, OR 97219
(503) 246-7737 | www.fryertuckchicken.com

Yes, its two restaurants in one! Forget about KFC, this is where it's at! Authentic fried chicken with all the fixin's. If you like old school atmosphere and top-notch quality, then this is the place for you. Your kids will notice the difference when they take their first bite.

LITTLE RIVER CAFÉ

Southwest Portland

0315 SW Montgomery St. Ste. 310
Portland, OR 97201
(503) 227-2327

Waterfront views, great sandwiches, and Umpqua ice cream team up to make this Southwest charmer the place to be!

MANDARIN PALACE

Southwest Portland

9225 SW Allen Rd.
Portland, OR 97223
(503) 245-2775 | www.mandarin-palace.com

Delicious Cantonese-style Chinese food in Southwest Portland. Whether you're dining in or just picking up some take-out, the staff at Mandarin is always quick with a smile...and your food. The egg-rolls are crisp, crunchy perfection, and the Barbecued Pork Lo Mein is spot-on. Soups and noodle dishes are generously loaded with meat, chicken, or fish. Perfect for a night out with the kids!

NEW YORK, NEW YORK

Southwest Portland

7737 SW Barbur Blvd.
Portland, OR 97219
(503) 768-4408

Old school Italian food; some of the best New York-style pizza in the Portland area. Ravioli, eggplant and chicken parmigiana, and spaghetti and meatballs are all delizioso!

NOAH'S BAGELS
Southwest Portland

6366 SW Capitol Hwy.
Portland, OR 97239
(503) 293-3183 | www.noahs.com

Grab a bagel and a schmear here. The perfect pit stop to fill 'er up and go. Hot soups and fresh salads, bagel dogs and pizza bagels, bagels and lox are all delicious, healthy, and kid-friendly.

OLD MARKET PUB & BREWERY
Southwest Portland

6959 SW Multnomah Blvd.
Portland, OR 97223
(503) 244-2337 | www.drinkbeerhere.com

This place is just made for kids and dads with fun, healthy and not so healthy food, and some of the best beer in town. Kids will love the grilled 3-Cheese Quesadilla, 13 inches of melted, cheesy goodness. Send them over the Moon with the "Big Bad Brownie" or the "Cookie Monster & Ice Cream" desserts. Dad can choose from over a dozen beers, plus seasonal and rotating guest taps. Try the Hot Tamale beer, brewed with jalapeno and Serrano peppers, with the Nachos Chili Con Carne for a fiery hot treat.

PHO NGUYEN
Southwest Portland

4795 SW 77th Ave.
Portland, OR 97225
(503) 297-3389

Fresh ingredients combined with speedy, friendly service makes this Raleigh Hills Pho establishment a top choice for Portland dads. If your kids are willing to try something a bit different, they will become Pho fans for life. The rich, aromatic, deeply flavorful broth and the crispy crunch of the bean sprouts perfectly compliment the warm comfort of the meat.

RALEIGH HILLS PUB
Southwest Portland

4495 SW Scholls Ferry Rd.
Portland, OR 97225
(503) 292-1723 | www.mcmenamins.com

Try the African Chicken Peanut Soup on Wednesdays, so tasty you'll plan your week around it! Kids love the Scooby Snacks and Tater Tots. The Hammerhead Garden Burger is almost criminally delicious, a perfect union of Hammerhead Ale & Malted Grain.

SALVADOR MOLLY'S
Southwest Portland

1523 SW Sunset Blvd
Portland, OR 97239
(503) 293-1790 | www.salvadormollys.com

Featuring food from around the globe, Salvador Molly's has fun items for kids, like Pirate's Coconut Shrimp Stix and Dino Nuggets, dinosaur-shaped chicken nuggets.

33

THE OLD SPAGHETTI FACTORY
Southwest Portland

0715 Bancroft St.
Portland, OR 97239
(503) 222-5375 | www.osf.com

On the banks of the Willamette, the flagship restaurant of the Spaghetti factory features gorgeous views, family fun atmosphere, and food that will please your kids and your wallet. Check out the Mizithra Cheese and Browned Butter pasta dish; renowned to be a favorite dish of Homer while he composed the "Iliad."

BYWAYS CAFÉ
The Pearl District

1212 NW Glisan St.
Portland, OR 97209
(503) 221-0011 | www.bywayscafe.com

With its "travel the USA" theme, and quite possibly the best turkey burger in town, this authentic diner is very kid–friendly. Featuring hand-made shakes and homemade pies, the staff will make you feel like family. The décor, consisting of travel memorabilia from all fifty states, is the perfect match for the classic American fare served up with love at Byways. Try the Pendleton Melt: roast beef, BBQ Sauce, grilled onions, and cheddar cheese on grilled sourdough or the Hood River Chicken Sandwich, the best pairing of chicken and apples this side of the Gorge.

DESCHUTES BREWERY & PUBLIC HOUSE
The Pearl District

210 NW 11th Ave.
Portland, OR 97209
(503) 296-4906 | www.deschutesbrewery.com

Great food & drink in an inviting space loosely based on the design of a Scottish pub. Your kids will love the Large House-Baked Pretzel and the burgers and fries. Dads and more adventurous kids will be in Pacific Northwest Big Game Heaven. Think Elk Burgers, Obsidian Stout Venison Stew, and Buffalo Stroganoff! Plus, don't forget the many pub exclusive brews available in addition to their standard beers, like the legendary Black Butte Porter.

HOTLIPS PIZZA
The Pearl District

721 NW 9th Ave. #150
Portland, OR 97209
(503) 595-2342 | www.hotlipspizza.com

With its emphasis on local ingredients, sustainable methods, and tasty real fruit sodas made with seasonally available fruits and berries, you can feel good about taking your kids to eat at Hotlips.

P.F. CHANG'S BISTRO

The Pearl District

1139 NW Couch St.
Portland, OR 97209
(503) 432-4000 | www.pfchangs.com

Classic Chinese-American fare, with plenty to please the kids and dad. Don't miss the delectable spare ribs or the expertly prepared Lo Mein.

THE DAILY CAFÉ

The Pearl District

902 NW 13th Ave.
Portland, OR 97209
(503) 242-1916 | www.dailycafe.net

Seasonal foods, fresh ingredients, and reasonable prices join forces to make this Pearl Café a sure thing. The grilled cheese or the pb & marionberry on brioche will please the kiddies. Dads will dig the ruben panini or the tarragon chicken salad sandwich.

RESTAURANTS

35

THE BEST DAD/CHILD
ACTIVITIES

ALBERTA STREET FAIR
Alberta

Annually the third Saturday in August.
NE Alberta St. between NE 10th & 30th Ave.

Music, food, and fun! Check out the kid's area and march in the parade. See fire-eaters, stilt walkers, clowns, and all that keeps Portland weird!

DOVETAIL BAKERY
Alberta

3039 NE Alberta St.
Portland, OR 97211
(503) 287-0601 | www.dovetailbakery.blogspot.com

Chocolate chip cookies and scones that are so yummy, you won't believe they're all vegan.

FIRST THURSDAY DOWNTOWN PORTLAND
Downtown

www.firstthursdayportland.com

A great family activity! Walk through downtown, Old Town and the Pearl District and view art from dozens of galleries, or eat some cheese, drink some wine and listen to the chorus of the crowd blending with the sounds of local musicians and singers. Watch the street performers and visit with the many local artisans offering a wide array of hand-made crafts and jewelry, and view the truly amazing art for sale inside the galleries.

MULTNOMAH COUNTY LIBRARY CENTRAL BRANCH
Downtown

801 SW 10th Ave.
Portland, OR 97205
(503) 988-5123 | www.multcolib.org

The Central Library Branch, first opened in 1913, ranks second in the U.S. in overall circulation and first in the nation in circulation among libraries serving cities with under a million people. Portlanders are a book-loving people and no place in the city better embodies this sentiment than the "Main Branch," as it is sometimes referred to. The art and architecture are inspiring and the books are thoughtfully chosen by the dedicated staff. Be sure to show your children the Solar System Globes on the second floor. Check website for story-times.

NOON TUNES PIONEER SQUARE
Downtown

www.pioneercourthousesquare.org

Free hour-long concerts featuring the best local bands in Pioneer Courthouse Square. Enjoy free organic iced tea as you delight in the sights and sounds in Portland's "living room."

OREGON MARITIME MUSEUM
Downtown

Tom McCall Waterfront Park
(503) 224-7724 | www.oregonmaritimemuseum.org

Take a tour of the sternwheeler Portland the last steam-powered stern wheel tugboat still in operating in the U.S. The friendly docent will give your kids an informative tour of the ship. Touch and play with actual turn of the 20th Century artifacts and even blow a ship's whistle in the Children's Corner. Visit the library to see some wonderful books on the Pacific Northwest's rich and colorful nautical history. Afterward, stop at the gift shop for a souvenir.

OREGON NIKKEI LEGACY CENTER
Downtown

Japanese American History Museum
121 NW 2nd Ave.
Portland, OR 97209
(503) 224-1458 | www.oregonnikkei.org

Learn about the Nikkei or Japanese immigrants who were the first to call Portland their home. Explore the history of a people with your kids as you examine permanent and rotating exhibits chronicling a story of opportunity, discrimination, and success.

PORTLAND ART MUSEUM
Downtown

1219 SW Park Ave.
Portland, OR 97205
(503) 226-2811 | www.portlandartmuseum.org

At the oldest art museum on the West Coast kids under 17 are free! Share the world's great art with your kids. Be sure to visit the Confederated Tribes of Grande Ronde Center for Native American Art. Kids really respond to the thousands of prehistoric artifacts on display, especially the transformation masks made by the coastal tribes of the Pacific Northwest. Plus, tons of family & children's events, including special family tours of the museum accompanied by a kid-friendly docent.

PORTLAND FARMERS MARKET AT PORTLAND STATE UNIVERSITY
Downtown

www.portlandfarmersmarket.org

Takes place in the South Park Blocks between SW Hall & SW Montgomery Street. Features the best local produce, meat, seafood, cheese, and specialty foods and offers educational programs, such as Kids Cook at the Market, where your little cook can learn how to prepare simple, healthy meals made with local and seasonally available ingredients. Kids get to meet the farmers who grow and raise their food, and get a guided market tour!

PORTLAND ROSE FESTIVAL
Downtown

www.rosefestival.org

Each June the people of Portland come out for the Grand Floral Parade and to see who will be crowned Rose Queen. The Junior Rose Festival is the world's largest children's parade.

39

PORTLAND SATURDAY MARKET   Downtown

www.portlandsaturdaymarket.com

For over thirty-five years, the Portland Saturday Market has brought the very best in hand-crafted local goods to the people. From its new home in Tom McCall Waterfront Park, Portlanders gather to stroll along the river, run into old friends, sample delicious local food from the vendors, and do a little weekend shopping. Find cool clothes for your kids, like tie-dye Oregon State Beavers and Oregon Ducks baby and toddler clothes, or hand woven scarves from Touch the Sky or daring hand painted t-shirts from Wardrobe Ink. Saturday Market is a great place to people watch or just hang out. Listen to local musicians, watch the street performers, and witness the comings and goings of hippies, hipsters, rollerbladers, families, and all of their doggie companions. The food selection at Saturday Market ranges across regions and ethnicities. Try Greek, Lebanese, Polish, Creole, Nepalese, Guatemalan, Mexican, East African, and Asian cuisines or stick with the tried and true like Old Town Burgers or Portland's Elephant Ears. This being Portland means there are plenty of cold local brews to quaff in the sunshine, or rain, plus fair trade, organic coffee and espresso to go with your kettle corn or the wide variety of fresh-baked goodness and hand dipped chocolates available.

PORTLAND SPIRIT   Downtown

(503) 224-3900 | www.portlandspirit.com

Sail from Portland to Oregon City and back again in about three hours. Enjoy spectacular views of the Willamette River while savoring classic Pacific Northwest Cuisine. Your kids will love it!

PORTLAND VINTAGE TROLLEY   Downtown

(503) 323-7363 | www.vintagetrolleys.com

Take a ride in a replica 1904 Portland Streetcar. A roundtrip between Union Station and PSU takes about thirty minutes.

PORTLANDIA   Downtown

The Portland Building
1120 SW 5th Ave.
Portland, OR 97204

See the second largest hammered copper statue in the U.S. Only the Statue of Liberty is larger. At 36 feet tall and weighing in at six and a half tons, this lady is no one to mess with.

THE BITE OF OREGON   Downtown

www.biteoforegon.com
Held on the second weekend of August in Waterfront Park.

Features food from the best restaurants and food carts in town in a fun outdoor festival setting. Imbibe the finest craft beers at the Oregon Craft Beer Gardens or enjoy some of Oregon's finest wines at the MIX Wine Pavilion adjacent to the Gerry Frank's Oregon Chef Stage. Conclude your visit to the Bite with a visit to the Dessert Pavilion.

VOODOO DONUT
Downtown

22 SW 3rd Ave.
Portland, OR 97204
(503) 241-4704 | www.voodoodoughnut.com

Crazy doughnuts keep Portland weird! Kids will flip for the Captain My Captain and the Loop. Both are covered in vanilla frosting, but one is covered in Captain Crunch and the other is covered in Froot Loops. There are doughnuts covered in cocoa puffs, Tang flavored doughnuts, and even a Bubble Gum flavored doughnut called Dubble Bubble, that comes topped with an actual piece of Dubble Bubble Bubble Gum.

WATERFRONT BLUES FESTIVAL
Downtown

Tom McCall Waterfront Park, Annually from July 1st to 4th
www.waterfrontbluesfest.com

Top blues acts perform on the banks of the Willamette river to benefit the Oregon Food Bank. Bring some canned goods, and enjoy food, music, and fun for the whole family.

HAWTHORNE STREET FAIR
Hawthorne/Belmont

Between 30th and 50th Ave. in Mid August.

The kids' area is at Kids at Heart Toys at 3445 SE Hawthorne Blvd. Portland, OR 97214. Face painting, sing-alongs, puppet show, live music and more, await your kids at the Hawthorne Street Fair.

POWELL'S BOOKS ON HAWTHORNE
Hawthorne/Belmont

3723 SE Hawthorne Blvd
Portland, OR 97214
(503) 228-4561 | www.powells.com

Cozier and more intimate than the vast downtown branch, Hawthorne's branch of Powell's Books boasts an expansive children's section and a truly cosmic science fiction selection.

KIDS SUMMER COMIC WORKSHOP AT COSMIC MONKEY COMICS
Hollywood

(503) 453-5839

On Sundays June 20th through August 22 Cosmic Monkey gives those kids who fill all their school notebooks with superhero sketches a chance to really explore that talent.

THE HOLLYWOOD THEATER
Hollywood

4122 NE Sandy Blvd
Portland, OR 97212
(503) 281-4215 | www.filmaction.org

Built in 1926, the Hollywood Theater was originally both a vaudeville house and a movie theater. Cheap prices, great popcorn, and beautiful roaring twenties architecture make this a night at the movies they won't soon forget!

41

LLOYD CENTER ICE RINK Irvington/Lloyd District

953 Lloyd Center
Portland, OR 97232
(503) 288-6073 | www.lloydcenterice.com

Skate at the rink where Tonya Harding got her start! Just no Olympic reenactments please! Located inside Lloyd Center Mall, the rink offers lessons, a pro shop, birthday parties, their summer "Kool Kamp" and even broomball. What's broomball, you say? Just picture ice hockey played with broomsticks!

LAURELHURST THEATER AND PUB Laurelhurst

2735 E Burnside St.
Portland, OR 97214
(503) 232-5511 | www.laurelhursttheater.com

This historic art deco theater has been operating continuously in the same location since 1923. Enjoy pizza and a local microbrew with your film and popcorn and candy for the kids. Classic and current films are shown with admission for kids 12 and under going for the low, low price of $1!

MT. TABOR PARK Mt. Tabor

SE 60th Ave. & Salmon St.
Portland, OR 97215

Mt. Tabor Doggie Challenge Kid's Half Miler run/walk held each year in late July. Bring your four-legged friends and get the wiggles out with your kids and pups, then check out the live music and great food after.

PDX ADULT SOAPBOX DERBY/MT. TABOR Mt. Tabor

www.soapboxracer.com`

Come on out with the kids and watch a truly unique Portland tradition. Yes, a soapbox derby for grown-ups! Watch the teams compete against one another in categories such as speed, engineering, and crowd pleaser. Look out for a kids' version coming 2011.

MULTNOMAH DAYS Mt. Tabor

Annually in Mid August

March in Multnomah Days Parade led by the Chief of Police, see shiny red fire trucks, watch the fabulous floats, and delight in the frolicking clowns. The Get a Life Marching Band will be there to keep the people movin' and groovin' to the beat. The Kid Zone is located in the Multnomah Arts Center Parking Lot in Multnomah Village. With so many interactive exhibits, this event will quickly become a family favorite. Face painting and mask making, a rock climbing wall and a bouncy rocket are all part of the fun of this very family-friendly event. Check out the sidewalk sale to see the handiwork of local artisans. Local bands rock the scene and a food court and wine and beer garden present the best in local food and grog.

42

FIRST FRIDAY IN THE VILLAGE
Multnomah Village

Multnomah Village at Capitol Hwy. between
SW 33rd and 36th St. and adjoining streets
(503) 244-9683 | www.multnomahvillage.org

Listen to live music, check out the local art scene on the artwalk, and fun and festivities for the kiddies.

PORTLAND PIRATE FESTIVAL
North Portland

Annually, third weekend in September.
Cathedral Park, North Edison St. and Pittsbugh Ave.
Portland, OR 97203
www.portlandpiratefestival.com

Gather yer gold doubloons and set a course for adventure this September in Cathedral Park. Live music, jugglers, gypsies, and of course parrots make this a day to remember for any scurvy dog. Catch the live historical reenactments complete with swordplay and cannon battles! Crafts, rides, and puppet shows just for the kiddies!

STUMPTOWN COMIC FEST
North Portland

Doubletree Hotel
1000 NE Multnomah St.
Portland, OR 97232
www.stumptowncomics.com

The biggest comic festival in Portland feels intimate when compared with behemoths like Comic-Con.

FIFTY LICKS
Northeast Portland

E Burnside St. & Seventh Ave.
(954) 294-8868 | www.facebook.com/pages/Fifty-Licks-Ice-Cream/

With flavors like Tahitian Vanilla and Maple with Bacon... mmm...bacon, you'll be in heaven at this Portland food cart. Just keep the kids away from the Slabtown Whiskey ice cream.

GIUSTO FARMS
Northeast Portland

3518 NE 162nd Ave.
Portland, OR 92730
(503) 253-0271 | www.tricountyfarm.org

This urban farm has a small produce stand open from July all the way through February.

ACTIVITIES

43

GREEKFEST

Northeast Portland

First Weekend in October
3131 NE Glisan St.
Portland, OR 97232
www.goholytrinity.org

15,000 people a year attend the annual Greek Fest, a celebration of culture, food, dance, and music. From the people who brought you the concept of democracy and the delights of Western civilization, share some food, fun, and laughs. Imported and local food, cooking lessons, imported crafts, gifts, and jewelry from Greece, and a special Children's Corner make this an unforgettable event for the whole family. Puppet shows, coloring, games, face painting, and so much more are available for the kids. Make an ivy wreath or a gold medal for your little Olympian.

HELEN BERNHARD BAKERY

Northeast Portland

1717 NE Broadway
Portland, OR 97232
(503) 287-1251 | www.helenbarnhardbakery.com

Operating continuously and in the current location since 1939, this Portland Bakery serves up fresh baked goods with love. Breads, pastries, Danish, cupcakes, scones, muffins and cookies, are all baked on the premises, as are their unique and whimsical birthday and special occasion cakes. Check out their hyper-realistic Barbie cake for your little princess's next birthday.

ROSE'S ICE CREAM

Northeast Portland

5011 NE 42nd Ave.
Portland, OR 97218
(503) 256-3333

Enjoy homemade ice cream, milkshakes, ice cream sodas, ice cream sandwiches, malts, sundaes, and banana splits.

RUBY JEWEL SCOOPS ICE CREAM

Northeast Portland

3713 N Mississippi Ave.
Portland, OR 9227
(503) 505-9314 | www.rubyjewel.net

Maybe the best ice cream sandwiches in town, everything at Ruby's is local, sustainable, and delicious!

THE PLAYGROUND GYM
Northeast Portland

505 NE Grand Ave.
Portland, OR 97232
(503) 235-7529 | www.theplaygroundgym.com

Finally, a gym just for kids! Featuring a large matted play area, a cork dance and yoga floor, a climbing wall, an indoor tree house, and climbing ropes, all supervised by a stellar team of coaches. Classes are provided for Explorers; ages 1 to 3, Rockers; ages 3 to 5, and Rollers; ages 5-8. Gymnastics and Martial Arts classes are offered for children between the ages of four and twelve.

WORDSTOCK BOOK FAIR
Northeast Portland

Held in early October
Oregon Convention Center
777 NE MLK Jr. Blvd
www.wordstockfestival.com

Portland's annual book and writing fair is free for kids 13 and under. There is a dedicated children's section and a children's literature stage. Open their young minds to new ideas and possibilities at Portland's premier festival of books.

ALOTTO GELATO
NEIGHBORHOOD GELATERIA
Northwest

931 NW 23rd Ave.
Portland, OR 97210
(503) 228-1709 | www.alottogelato.biz

Made with care using local fruit, Alotto Gelato is a fun place to cool off any time of year. Some of the flavors offered are pretty offbeat but always delicious. In the past they have experimented with Guinness Stout, Sweet Corn, and even Olive Oil gelato. Some of the gelatos available currently include Champagne, Chocolate Chipotle, and Peanut Butter & Jelly.

BLISS CUPCAKES
Northwest

4708 NW Bethany Blvd.
Portland, OR 97229
(503) 645-6000 | www.blisscupcakeshop.com

Delicious cupcakes baked fresh each day, plus cookies, and Tillamook Ice Cream. Cupcake flavors rotate daily, but some of the standouts are the Red Velvet Bliss, Triple Chocolate, and Rainbow Bliss, a vanilla bean cake stuffed with sprinkles, topped with vanilla butter cream and rolled in mini M&M's.

CUPCAKE JONES
Northwest

307 NW 10th Ave.
Portland, OR 97209
(503) 222-4404 | www.cupcakejones.net

Every child's dream. A store devoted entirely to, you guessed it, cupcakes. Try the Pearl White velvet cake filled with vanilla bean pastry cream, topped with vanilla butter cream icing and a white chocolate pearl. These are serious gourmet cupcakes that even dad will love. Do not miss!

45

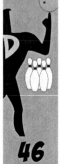

ACTIVITIES

KRUGER'S FARM MARKET

Northwest

17100 NW Sauvie Island Rd.
Portland, OR 97231
(503) 621-3489 | www.krugersfarmmarket.com

Head on over to Farmer Don Kruger's farm for family fun. Concerts each Thursday at 6pm, a great place for birthdays and picnics, pick your own produce, and for a real treat, try the farm-to-plate dinner. It doesn't get any more local or sustainable than this!

MIO GELATO

Northwest

25 NW 11th Ave.
Portland, OR 97209
(503) 226-8002 | www.mio-gelato.com

Traditional Italian gelato, espresso, and Italian hot chocolate. Made with hormone-free local milk and sustainable preparation methods.

NORTHWEST CHILDREN'S THEATER AND SCHOOL

Northwest

1819 NW Everett St.
Portland, OR 97209
(503) 222-2190 | www.nwcts.org

A non-profit theater group dedicated to children. Come see a show in their 450 seat theater located in the NW Neighborhood Cultural Center. Past shows have included adaptations of P.D. Eastman's book, "Go, Dog, Go."

OREGON JEWISH MUSEUM

Northwest

1953 NW Kearney St.
Portland, OR 97209
(503) 226-3600 | www.ojm.org

The only Jewish Museum in the Pacific Northwest, OJM features rotating exhibits as well as a research library and archive. A repository for documents and artifacts of Oregon's Jews, this museum makes for a nice family outing. Exhibits may focus on local Jewish art or history.

PITTOCK MANSION

Northwest

3229 NW Pittock Dr.
Portland, OR 97210
(503) 823-3623 | www.pittockmansion.org

Visit a 1914 French Renaissance chateau in the West Hills of Portland. Explore the twenty-two rooms on forty-six acres of land overlooking downtown Portland. The 1,000 foot elevation of the Pittock Mansion guarantees an abundance of bird species and spectacular views of downtown Portland and beyond.

TWO TARTS BAKERY INC.   Northwest

2309 NW Kearney St.
Portland, OR 97210
(503) 312-9522 | www.tartnation.wordpress.com
Your kids will flip for the tasty treats at Two Tarts Bakery. There is a wide variety of cookies to choose from, as well as brownies and bars. Try the Apple Gems, Tart Lemon Thumbprints and the Lil' Mama. Follow the bakery on Two Tarts Bakery Blog at www.tartnation.wordpress.com.

FIRST SUNDAY IN   Old Town/Chinatown
OLD TOWN

Self-guided tour: Follow the bronze plaques in the sidewalk of 3rd and 4th Avenues and learn about the history and people that have called Old Town home over the generations. For a guided eco-tour call (503) 733-4222.

GUAPO COMICS & COFFEE Southeast Portland

6350 SE Foster Rd.
Portland, OR 97206
503.772.3638 | www.guapocomicsandbooks.com
This hip comic store believes there's a comic out there even your mother would love, and they have a selection wide enough that they just might prove it.

OBONFEST   Southeast Portland

Annually in August
3720 SE 34th Ave.
Portland, OR 97202
(503) 234-9456 | www.oregonbuddhisttemple.com
Honor your ancestors by participating in this annual Japanese festival. Thrill to the pulsating rhythms of Portland Taiko. Join with the community in the closing dances and sample some delicious Japanese cuisine.

OREGON MUSEUM OF SCIENCE AND INDUSTRY

Southeast Portland

1945 SE Water Ave.
Portland, OR 97214
(503) 797-4000 | www.omsi.edu

If your kids are captivated by science, technology, and the world of tomorrow, then take them down to Oregon's Museum of Science and Industry. Located on the east bank of the Willamette River, OMSI offers world class rotating and permanent science exhibitions, an IMAX Dome theater, a top-notch planetarium, and an expansive kids section on the second floor. A retired naval submarine, the U.S.S. Blueback, floats majestically on the Willamette River outside the museum. Tours are available daily as are Summer Camp-In sleepovers for kids in grades 3 and up. See science documentaries and first run kids movies on the jaw-droppingly massive OMNI-MAX Dome screen. Your kids will be awed by the scale of this impressive piece of technology. Full dome video in the Harry C. Kendall Planetarium will whisk your kids away to distant planets and galaxies. Summer Science camps and classes are unmatched in scope and quality. They include trips to the Oregon Coast, the Cascades, and even the John Day Fossil Beds National Monument. Perhaps your little will one will discover a new dinosaur species! The OMSI Market, OMSI's café, is a step up from the industrial cafeteria food of most museum shops. Plenty of healthy, vegetarian, and vegan options.

PIX PATISSERIE

Southeast Portland

3402 SE Division St.
Portland, OR 97202
(503) 232-4407 | www.pixpatisserie.com

Pastry chef Cheryl Wakerhauser studied to be an astronaut before mastering the pastry arts in Southern France. Now she explores the final frontier of fun as she delights children of all ages with her tasty treats. Try the Shazam! Rich caramel mousse meets decadent chocolate almond cake resulting in a truly cosmic explosion of flavors. Or sample the Tiki Tiki, a mango/passion fruit mousse with coconut meringue and almond cake topped with fresh fruit, that looks much like Spongebob Squarepants's Pineapple House.

KEANAS CANDYLAND

Sellwood/Westmoreland

5314 SE Milwaukie Ave.
Portland, OR 97202
(503) 235-5177

A bakery, candy store, and restaurant. Looking like something straight out of Hansel and Gretel, this shop is covered from stem to stern in faux gingerbread, candy canes, and features a jelly bean walkway. Dinner is by reservation only.

OAKS AMUSEMENT PARK Sellwood/Westmoreland

7805 SE Oaks Park Way
Portland, OR 97202
(503) 233-5777 | www.oakspark.com

Just a 3-mile drive from downtown, Oaks Park is a great place to take your kids for a day of family fun. For over one hundred years, Oaks Park has entertained with rides, games, and other attractions, plus food vendors and a picnic area. Skate to the sounds of a Wurlitzer pipe organ at the Oaks Park Rollerskating Rink. Try the kiddie rides, including the balloon ride, bouncing frog, and the big slide. Plus bumper cars, roller coasters, and Ferris wheels for the bigger kids.

SELLWOOD COMMUNITY CENTER Sellwood/Westmoreland

1436 SE Spokane St.
Portland, OR 97202
(503) 823-3195 | www.portlandonline.com

A great place for kids. Features a gymnasium, a basketball court and a playground, but the real draw is the many camps and classes. Classes at the Center include parent/child music and art classes and parent/child science and nature classes. Other fun classes are Tiny-Tot Yoga and Baby Play/ Toddler Gym. In the Fall, don't miss the Halloween Carnival.

ALPENROSE DAIRY TOUR Southwest

6149 SW Shattuck Rd.
Portland, OR 97221
(503) 244-1133 | www.alpenrose.com

Alpenrose is practically a city unto itself and is bristling with amenities. There is Alpenrose stadium, three baseball/softball fields, an opera house, the Alpenrose Velodrome; an Olympic style bicycle track, a pony barn, a quarter midget racing track, and Dairyville, an authentic recreation of a frontier town straight out of the Old West. Don't miss the old-fashioned ice-cream parlor selling delicious Alpenrose Ice Cream. In the spring, the dairy holds one the best Easter egg hunts around.

CELEBRATE THE SENSES Southwest

1509 SW Sunset Blvd. Ste. 1K
Portland, OR 97239
(503) 810-0275 | www.celebratethesenses.com

This is the rare place that offers full service yoga for the whole family, with classes and workshops for children, teens and adults.

49

ACTIVITIES

OREGON ZOO
Southwest

4001 SW Canyon Rd.
Portland, OR 97221
(503) 226-1561 | www.oregonzoo.org

Home to the world's most successful elephant breeding programs, in addition to being a world-class zoo, the Oregon Zoo hosts an outdoor summer concert series featuring top name talent. Bring a blanket, a picnic basket, and dance the night away. In the winter see the Zoo Lights holiday light show. Ride the train, meet Rudolph, and walk amongst the dazzling lights.

PORTLAND CHILDREN'S MUSEUM
Southwest

4015 SW Canyon Rd.
Portland, OR 97221
(503) 223-6500 | www.portlandcm.org

The sixth oldest children's museum in the country provides multiple environments for your young explorers. The Building Bridgetown exhibit will inspire your budding architect or future construction worker to build the city of tomorrow. The Pet Hospital is perfect for your little animal lover. After all that hard work why not head over to the Grasshopper Grocery and Bistro to do the grocery shopping and "cook" a meal for dad. A pretend grocery store complete with shopping carts and pretend food. Your child can either "shop" or ring the groceries up. In the Bistro there is a pretend kitchen for the kids and seating for dad to enjoy a delicious, home cooked meal.

BEN & JERRY'S PORTLAND PEARL DISTRICT SCOOP SHOP
The Pearl District

301 NW 10th St.
Portland, OR 97209
(503) 796-3033 | www.benjerry.com/pearldistrict/menu

America's favorite ice cream from Vermont is now available in the Pearl. Try a frozen Latte made with fair trade coffee and treat the tots to a cone, a shake, or a sundae made with Ben & Jerry's unbeatable ice cream.

COOL MOON ICE CREAM
The Pearl District

1105 NW Johnson St.
Portland, OR 97209
(503) 224-2021 | www.coolmoonicecream.com

Unique flavors set this ice cream shop apart from all other. Lemon lavender, buttermilk marion berry swirl, and kulfi, are just a few of the unusual offerings at Cool Moon.

OREGON CHILDREN'S THEATER The Pearl District

600 SW 10th St. Ste. 313
Portland, OR 97205
(503) 228-9571 | www.octc.org

Watch local kids act in some of the best local theater productions around, or better yet enroll your children in their excellent classes at Oregon Acting Academy.

PLAYDATE PDX The Pearl District

1434 NW 17th St.
Portland, OR 97209
(503) 227-PLAY | www.playdatepdx.com

A 7,500 square foot indoor play structure, serving food and Stumptown Coffee.

PORTLAND STREETCAR The Pearl District

www.portlandstreetcar.org

A four mile streetcar line in downtown Portland is a fun way to see the sights of the city with your kids.

SAHAGUN HANDMADE CHOCOLATES The Pearl District

10 NW 16th Ave.
Portland, OR 97209
(503) 274-7065 | www.sahagunchocolates.com

Perfect for that special day out with the kids or a rainy afternoon pick-me-up. Try hot chocolate made with real melted single origin chocolate and organic milk. The handmade chocolates and caramels are top notch and the Iced Chocolate will make any sunny day even sunnier!

ACTIVITIES

THE BEST DAD/CHILD
STORES

STORES

ALBERTA FOOD CO-OP

Alberta

1500 NE Alberta St.
Portland, OR 97211
(503) 287-4333 | www.albertagrocery.coop
Started in 1997 by neighbors who banded together to secure low cost, high quality organic food, the co-op became successful enough to open the Alberta Cooperative Grocery in 2001. In addition to being a great source of local healthy food, there is a wonderful play corner with custom-built cabinets and plenty of toys and books.

GRASSHOPPER

Alberta

1816 NE Alberta St.
Portland, OR 97211
(503) 335-3131 | www.grasshopperstore.com
Truly a unique children's store in NE Portland, with a focus on organic clothing, American made products, and non-toxic toys, as well as an extensive children's book collection from yesterday and today.

GREEN BEAN BOOKS

Alberta

1600 NE Alberta St.
Portland, OR 97211
(503) 954-2354 | www.greenbeanbookspdx.com
Independent children's bookstore selling new and used books in a bright, cheerful atmosphere. Read a book to your kids on a comfy couch or under their "magical draping tree." Vending machines offer items such as finger puppets and temporary tattoos. Stop in for story time every Tuesday morning at 11am.

MIMOSA

Alberta

1718 NE Alberta Ave.
Portland, OR 97211
(503) 288-0770 | www.mimosa-studios.com
Paint your own pottery studio for kids and adults. Open to all skill levels. You select a piece of unfinished pottery and paint it yourself. The studio fires it up in the kiln and you pick it up a few days later. Your kids will be so proud of their handiwork.

BILLY GALAXY

Downtown

912 W. Burnside St.
Portland, OR 97209
(503) 227-8253 | www.billygalaxy.com
All the toys your mom threw away while you were at sleepaway camp. Introduce your kids to the toys you played with when you were a kid.

CAMERON'S BOOKS AND MAGAZINES

Downtown

336 SW 3rd Ave.
Portland, OR 97204
(503) 228-2391 | www.cameronsbooks.com

Portland's oldest used bookstore. Piles of old Life, Look, and National Geographic magazines, plus thousands of quirky and out-of-print titles make Cameron's a great place for your kids to explore the past and pick up some bedtime books you're not likely to find anywhere else.

EVERYDAY MUSIC

Downtown

1313 W Burnside St.
Portland, OR 97209
(503) 274-0961 | www.everydaymusic.com

Massive library of over 100,000 new and used CDs and vinyl. EM also has a huge stock of DVDs and VHS. Own your children's favorite movies and television shows, or introduce them to the weird and wonderful cartoons of the past.

FINNEGAN'S TOYS & GIFTS INCORPORATED

Downtown

922 Yamhill St.
Portland, OR 97205
(503) 221-0306 | www.finneganstoys.com

The Pacific Northwest's largest independent toy store has been delighting area children for over thirty years.

GYMBOREE

Downtown

Pioneer Place Mall
700 SW 5th Ave. Zone C, Lower Level
Portland, OR 97204
(503) 224-2075| www.gymboree.com

Cool clothes for babies and kids, plus an extensive selection of Halloween costumes, toys, games, and books.

THE CHILDREN'S PLACE

Downtown

Pioneer Place Mall
700 SW 5th Ave. Zone A, Lower Level
Portland, OR 97204
(503) 222-1708 | www.childrensplace.com

Selling the very best in children's clothing and more for newborns, toddlers, and older kids, too.

SANRIO PIONEER PLACE   Downtown

700 SW 5th Ave.
Portland, OR 97204
(503) 295-7975 | www.sanrio.com

Hello Kitty Headquarters in the PDX! Don't let your princess be caught in the rain without a Hello Kitty umbrella! Be seen sipping water from your very own Hello Kitty Eco-Friendly Water Bottle! Mac and Cheese just tastes better when it's eaten out of a Hello Kitty heart-shaped bowl.

THE REAL MOTHER GOOSE   Downtown

901 SW Yamhill St.
Portland, OR 97205
(503) 223-9510 | www.therealmothergoose.com

For nearly forty years, The Real Mother Goose has showcased only the very best work produced by America's most talented artisans. Hand-crafted wooden games such as chess and checker sets, backgammon, and more are sure to provide your children with hours of fun.

AVALON THEATER/ELECTRIC   Hawthorne/Belmont
CASTLE'S WUNDERLAND

3451 SE Belmont St.
Portland, OR 97214
(503) 238-1617 | www.wunderlandgames.com/avalonnew.htm

Movie theater and arcade games for kids. Low prices for movies and refreshments make for an unbeatable bargain.

CD GAMEXCHANGE   Hawthorne/Belmont

1428 SE 36th St.
Portland, OR 97214
(503) 233-1708 | www.cdgamexchange.org

Buy, sell, or trade your CDs, DVDs, and video games. When kids are bored with their old music, movies, or games, take 'em down to CD Gamexchange for something new without spending a lot of green.

EXCALIBUR BOOKS   Hawthorne/Belmont
& COMICS

2444 SE Hawthorne Blvd
Portland, OR 97214
(503) 231-7351 | www.excaliburcomics.net

Portland's oldest comic book shop, in continuous operation since 1974.

HOLLYWOOD PORTLAND COSTUMERS
Hawthorne/Belmont

635 SE Hawthorne Blvd.
Portland, OR 97214

(503) 235-9215 | www.hollywoodportlandcostumers.com

In the business for fifty years, the folks at Hollywood Portland Costumers have been outfitting fantasists and dreamers for generations. Whether it's Halloween or the Oregon Country Fair, they can help your little guys pick out just the right costume.

KIDS AT HEART TOYS
Hawthorne/Belmont

3445 SE Hawthorne Blvd.
Portland, OR 97214

(503) 231-2954 | www.kidsathearttoys.com

With a commitment to fairly traded and sustainable toys, a thoughtful selection of books, and a love of children that shows in how they conduct their business, Kids at Heart Toys is a store that you can feel good about shopping at.

MOVIE MADNESS
Hawthorne/Belmont

4320 SE Belmont St.
Portland, OR 97215

(503) 234-4363 | www.moviemadnessvideo.com

With over 70,000 movies to choose from, Movie Madness brings all the magic of Hollywood together in one Portland location. Hands down, the most diverse selection of movies and television series on DVD and VHS available to rent in town, or maybe anywhere. Don't forget to visit "The Museum of Motion Picture History" while you're there. Over 100 objects and artifacts from Hollywood's storied past are presented here for your perusal, including the knife from Psycho, and models from Alien and Star Wars.

MUSE ART+DESIGN
Hawthorne/Belmont

4224 SE Hawthorne Blvd.
Portland, OR 97215

(503) 231-8704 | www.museartanddesign.com

Great source for art supplies for your little artists. Acrylic paints, oil colors, and watercolors, plus brushes, papers, and more.

PAPER MOON BOOKS
Hawthorne/Belmont

4707 SE Belmont St.
Portland, OR 97215

(503) 239-8848

A wide range of books, including children's literature, cookbooks, science, nature, history of the old West, humor and comics. Paper Moon also carries a wide assortment of ephemera such as historic photos, postcards, menus, and programs.

PRESENTS OF MIND
Hawthorne/Belmont

3633 SE Hawthorne Blvd.
Portland, OR 97214
(503) 230-7740 | www.presentsofmind.tv
The latest in hip baby clothes and gear, plus quirky gifts and cards.

SHADOWHOUSE COLLECTIBLES
Hawthorne/Belmont

4220 SE Hawthorne Blvd.
Portland, OR 97215
(503) 236-5005 | www.shadowhouse.net

Weird things from the past! Your children will love wandering through this strange collection of antiques and oddities. Old cameras, magazines, furniture, Native American art and photographs, and other archaic items will intrigue the young mind.

THE DOLLAR SCHOLAR
Hawthorne/Belmont

3343 SE Hawthorne Blvd.
Portland, OR 97214
(503) 235-2222 | www.thedollarscholar.net

This is not your standard issue dollar store. Cheesy old school gag gifts and toys are available for your perusal or purchase. Your kids will love the wild abandon of this decidedly non-corporate shop.

COSMIC MONKEY COMICS
Hollywood

5335 NE Sandy Blvd.
Portland, OR 97213
(503) 517-9050 | www.cosmicmonkeycomics.com

Cool comic shop selling a mix of new and older comics. Highly recommended are the comic drawing workshops and camps for kids between ages 5 and 17.

THINGS FROM ANOTHER WORLD
Hollywood

4133 NE Sandy Blvd.
Portland, OR 97214
(503) 284-4693 | www.tfaw.com

One stop shopping for role-playing toys, action figures, models, sculptures, collectibles, gaming cards, and comics. Superheroes, Star Wars, Star Trek, or anime, whatever your science fiction and fantasy needs are, it's all here.

STORES

AFRICAN RHYTHM TRADERS Irvington/Lloyd District

3904 NE MLK Jr. Blvd.
Portland, OR 97212
(503) 288-6950 | www.africanrhythmtraders.com
Give them the gift of pure joy. African hand drums will make their little hearts shine! Djembes, talking drums, and African bells and shakers will instill confidence and provide hours of fun.

BROADWAY BOOKS Irvington/Lloyd District

1714 NE Broadway
Portland, OR 97232
(503) 284-1726 | www.broadwaybooks.net
Independent booksellers since 1992, offering a diverse selection of children's literature and non-fiction.

F.Y.E. Irvington/Lloyd District

1236 Lloyd Ctr.
Portland, OR 97232
(503) 288-8797 | www.suncoast.com
The latest and the greatest in DVDs, collectibles, and more.

MIO GELATO Irvington/Lloyd District

2757 NE Pacific St.
Portland, OR 97212
(503) 288-4800 | www.mio-gelato.com
Serving up brightly colored, gleaming dishes of delight, this purveyor of authentic Italian gelato is a hit with the little folks, while the espresso bar will give dad that little lift he needs to keep up with the kids.

HOLLYWOOD VINTAGE Laurelhurst

2800 NE Sandy Blvd
Portland, OR 97232
(503) 233-1890 | www.hollywoodvintage.com
Great place to gear up for Halloween. They carry costumes, wigs, accessories, and tons of vintage hats and clothing.

MUSIC MILLENNIUM Laurelhurst

3158 E Burnside St.
Portland, OR 97214
(503) 231-8926 | www.musicmillennium.com
Portland's premier music and video store and the oldest continually operating record store in the Pacific Northwest. Show your kids how music was purchased before iTunes. Check out the free live performances by local and national acts. As their slogan says, Music Millennium is "a place where the music and people still matter."

STORES

ANNIE BLOOM'S BOOKS Multnomah Village

7834 SW Capitol Hwy.
Portland, OR 97219
(503) 246-0053 | www.annieblooms.com

For over thirty years, Annie Bloom's Books has been providing great literature to the citizens of Multnomah village and beyond. The knowledgeable, friendly staff is always ready to help you find what you are looking
for, or make a reading recommendation. A terrific children's book section has something for everyone, and lots of friendly furry hand puppets
would love to go home with you and your little guys.

SWEETS, ETC. Multnomah Village

7828 SW Capitol Hwy.
Portland, OR 97219
(503) 293-0088 | www.sweetsetc.com

Charming candy shop in the Village featuring chocolate from all over the
world, a wide variety of gummi products, jelly beans, and licorice. Stop by and
cool off with some Umpqua Ice Cream.

THINKER TOYS Multnomah Village

7784 SW Capitol Hwy.
Portland, OR 97219
(503) 245-3936 | www.thinkertoysoregon.com

Founded by two former Portland schoolteachers, Thinker Toys features a
knowledgeable, friendly staff and a diverse selection of toys. Chosen as
Portland's Best Toy Store for 2009 by Nickelodeon's ParentConnect.com.

BRIDGE CITY COMICS North Portland

3725 N. Mississippi Ave.
Portland, OR 97227
(503) 282-5484 | www.bridgecitycomics.com

Billing themselves as "Comics for the People," Bridge City offers the very
latest in new comics, plus new and used graphic novels and trade pa-
perbacks. Stock up on all your comic supplies and accessories too, such
as comic bags and backing boards.

GRAMMY AND NONNA'S TOYS North Portland

8621 N Lombard St.
Portland, OR 97203
(503) 432-8732 | www.grammyandnonnastoys.com

North Portland toy store with an emphasis on educational toys, as well as
wooden and non-electronic toys. They also sell toys made from recycled
materials.

MISSING LINK TOYS
North Portland

3824 N Mississippi Ave.
Portland, OR 97227
(503) 235-0032 | www.missinglinktoys.com

Large collection of vinyl toys, robot toys, and plush animals for the wee ones. There is an adjacent art gallery next to the store as well.

MISSISSIPPI TREE HOUSE
North Portland

3742 N Mississippi Ave.
Portland, OR 97227
(503) 928-5987 | www.misstreehouse.com

New and recycled clothing, bedding, clothes, toys, and art supplies, much of it locally sourced. Storytime and other family events are held in the playroom. Toddler Arts and Crafts Tuesdays and Musical Sing-along & Storytime with Tyleena are popular with parents and children alike.

A CHILDREN'S PLACE BOOKSTORE
Northeast Portland

4807 NE Fremont St.
Portland, OR 97213
(503) 284-8294 | www.achildrensplacebookstore.com

For over thirty years parents and kids have been making memories at this charming bookstore devoted entirely to kids. Your young readers will be in heaven as they wander the aisles in search of their next bedtime story. Visit A Children's Place for story times every Thursday at 10:30 am. Join them for their annual Sidewalk Chalk Party in August.

BELLA STELLA
Northeast Portland

2751 NE Broadway
Portland, OR 97232
(503) 284-4636 | www.bellastellababy.com

Pick up something for your little one, a baby-shower gift, or your wife, if you've got another on the way, at this shop that sells baby, toddler oand maternity clothes.

BLACK WAGON
Northeast Portland

3964 N Mississippi Ave.
Portland, OR 97227
(503) 916-0000 | www.blackwagon.com

Billing itself as "a modern boutique for babies and kids," Black Wagon is another Portland jewel. For the fashion forward dad or child, this is the place to shop. Unusual and hip toys, books, and clothing for the younger set. A complete selection of organic products, including toys, blankets, pillows, clothing, and more.

BRIDGETOWN HOBBIES & GAMES

Northeast Portland

3350 NE Sandy Blvd
Portland, OR 97232
(503) 234-1881 | www.bthobbies.com

Hobby supplies for less! Model rockets, pine wood racing cars, die-cast models, decals, paint, magazines and more for your lil' hobbyist.

CREATIVE KIDSTUFF

Northeast Portland

7000 NE Airport Way, Concourse C
Portland, OR 97218
(503) 288-6388 | www.creativekidstuff.com

Sells developmental and educational toys for kids of all ages. Whether its books, art supplies, stuffed animals, dolls, toy trucks, puzzles, or games, Creative Kidstuff has what you need.

LEARNING PALACE

Northeast Portland

9971 NE Cascades Pkwy.
Portland, OR 97220
(503) 251-1833 | www.learningpalace.com

Sells educational supplies, toys, books, puzzles, musical instruments, models and much more.

MILAGROS BOUTIQUE

Northeast Portland

5433 NE 30th Ave.
Portland, OR 97211
(503) 493-4141 | www.milagrosboutique.com

Vegan shoes, recycled toys, cloth diapers, and reusable swimmies...this is Portland!

POLLIWOG

Northeast Portland

234 NE 28th Ave.
Portland, OR 97232
(503) 236-3903 | www.polliwogportland.com

Toys and clothes for babies and kids at this adorably–named little shop.

POWELL'S BOOKS AT PDX   Northeast Portland

7000 NE Airport Way, Ste 2250
Portland, OR 97218

(503) 228-4651 | www.powells.com

Whether you're heading out of town for a trip or returning to the PDX, there is always something worth reading at Powell's PDX branch. There is even a fairly decent sized children's section, considering the goldilocks size of the store. Don't forget to stop at Coffee People PDX, the last bastion of a once mighty coffee shop empire, for as Portlanders know, books and beans go hand in hand!

THE KID'S EDGE   Northeast Portland

2200 NE Broadway St.
Portland, OR 97232

(503) 284-3343 | www.thekidsedge.com

Resale, overstock, and liquidation items for babies through teens. Consignment and resale shop featuring top brands and styles. The Kid's Edge also showcases local artists and musicians and gives them a space to present their efforts.

SERIOUS JUGGLING   Northeast Portland

2635 NE Broadway St., Ste 2
Portland, OR 97232

(503) 233-2577 | www.seriousjuggling.com

If you're serious about juggling, then this is the store for you. Come on in and see the extensive selection of juggling balls, juggling clubs, devil sticks, books, DVD's and more!

SHELBY'S WORLD OF WHEELS Northeast Portland
COLLECTIBLE TOY STORE

6063 NE Glisan St.
Portland, OR 97213

(503) 238-4444

Sells pre-1980 Hotwheels and Matchbox cars, Tonka Trucks, model kits, action figures, and much more.

63

STORES

TITLE WAVE USED BOOKSTORE

Northeast Portland

216 NE Knott St.
Portland, OR 97212
(503) 988-5021

Out of Circulation titles from the Multnomah County Library, with a vast children's section, especially non-fiction. There are books on every conceivable subject, plus VHS tapes, books on CD, and back issues of many popular magazines.

AUDUBON SOCIETY OF PORTLAND NATURE STORE

Northwest Portland

5151 NW Cornell Rd.
Portland, OR 97210
(503) 292-9453 | www.audubonportland.org

Offers a wide selection of nature books, bird feeders and houses, bird seed and suet, plus binoculars and spotting scopes.

CHILD'S PLAY

Northwest Portland

2305 NW Kearney St.
Portland, OR 97210
(503) 224-5586 | www.childsplayportland.com

A great little toy store in Northwest Portland, Child's Play has a truly awe-inspiring selection of plush animals to make your child smile. Lots of Melissa and Doug wooden toys, including fantastic pretend food play sets. There is also a nice little children's book section plus a large assortment of games, stickers, and more.

CHRISTMAS AT THE ZOO

Northwest Portland

118 NW 23rd Ave.
Portland, OR 97210
(503) 223-4048 | www.christmasatthezoo.com

It's always Christmastime at Christmas At The Zoo! Specializing in holiday ornaments and plush animals, this unique store is perfect for those with visions of sugar plums dancing in their heads.

DUCK DUCK GOOSE

Northwest Portland

517 NW 23rd Ave.
Portland, OR 97210
(503) 916-0636

Upscale baby and children's clothing for your little ones. Spoil them with clothes, pajamas, and blankets that will last long enough to become hand-me-downs.

MOONSTRUCK CHOCOLATE CAFÉ

Northwest Portland

526 NW 23rd Ave.
Portland, OR 97210
(503) 542-3400 | www.moonstruckchocolate.com

Kids will love this shop on a chilly winter day. Try the milkshakes, the hot chocolate, or the chocolate truffles in fanciful shapes, such as fish, moons, stars, and animals.

NORTHWEST SWEETS CANDIES AND SUCH

Northwest Portland

740 NW 23rd Ave.
Portland, OR 97210
(503) 360-1350 | www.nwsweets.com

Retro candy and treats. Share a memory with your kids. With Sugar Daddies, Smarties and Squirrel Nut Zippers, you're in classic candy paradise! Northwest Sweets also sells handmade caramels, a wide variety of licorice, salt water taffy, and caramel covered fruit in the fall.

FLOATING WORLD COMICS
Old Town/Chinatown

20 NW 5th Ave. #101
Portland, OR 97209
(503) 241-0227 | www.floatingworldcomics.com

Nice selection of mainstream and indie comics and graphic novels, to appeal to kids and dads alike. Cool toys for kids and grown-ups, too.

GROUND KONTROL CLASSIC ARCADE

Old Town/Chinatown

511 NW Couch St.
Portland, OR 97209
(503) 796-9364 | www.groundkontrol.com

Go back in time with your kids to the glorious 1980's. Challenge your progeny to a friendly game of Frogger, Donkey Kong, or Pac-Man. 21 and over after 5pm.

JUST BE COMPLEX AND COMPOUND GALLERY

Old Town/Chinatown

107 NW 5th Ave.
Portland, OR 97209
(503) 796-2733

Toys, including vinyl figures and plush toys.

STORES

LOOKING GLASS BOOKSTORE
Sellwood/Westmoreland

7983 SE 13th Ave.
Portland, OR 97202
(503) 227-4760 | www.lookingglassbookstore.com

This quaint Sellwood bookstore houses its children's section in a little red caboose and is presided over by a dog named Charlie.

SPIELWERK
Sellwood/Westmoreland

7956 SE 13th Ave.
Portland, OR 97202
(503) 736-3000 | www.spielwerktoys.com

Community toy store with a decidedly non-commercial bent. Focusing on hand crafted wooden toys, toys made with organic materials, and other unique toys to be found nowhere else in the city.

SPOILED ROTTEN
Sellwood/Westmoreland

1626 SE Bybee Blvd
Portland, OR 97202
(503) 234-7250

All you need for baby and toddler.

ACADEMY THEATER
Southeast Portland

7818 SE Stark St.
Portland, OR 97215
(503) 252-0500 | www.academytheaterpdx.com

Opened in 1948, entering the Academy Theater is a little like stepping back into the storied past of Tinsel Town. With some of the original elements in place, such as the restored lobby, and other portions lovingly rebuilt, such as the theater's marquee, the Academy is a great place to see a great movie. There are tasty treats such as Flying Pie Pizza, Nathan's Hot Dogs, and even sushi on sale at the lobby, plus old movie staples like popcorn, candy, and soda. Oh, and did I mention the ten microbrews on tap for Daddy?

ECO BABY GEAR
Southeast Portland

2122 SE Division St.
Portland, OR 97202
(503) 233-4167 | www.ecobabygear.com

Be kind to the Earth and buy only the most Earth-friendly products & gear for your baby.

FUTURE DREAMS BOOKS SCIENCE FICTION & COMIC ART BOOKSTORE
Southeast Portland

1847 East Burnside St., Ste 116
Portland, OR 97214
(503) 231-8311 | www.futuredreamstore.com

Your ticket to the best in science fiction, fantasy, and comics for over thirty years, Future Dreams carries a treasure trove of rare magazines and memorabilia. Great for a rainy day with the munchkins.

HAGGIS MCBAGGIS
Southeast Portland

6802 SE Milwaukie Ave.
Portland, OR 97202
(503) 234-0849

The best in kid's shoes in Portland. Top brands for sale at this whimsically named store.

LONGFELLOW'S BOOKS & MAGAZINES
Southeast Portland

1401 SE Division St.
Portland, OR 97202
(503) 239-5222 | www.longfellowspdx.com

Since 1980, Longfellow's has brought independence and diversity to Portland readers young and old. Strong selection of juvenile series for kids, with a special focus on Pacific Northwest history.

MOTHER NATURE'S EARTH FRIENDLY BABY PRODUCTS
Southeast Portland

2627 SE Clinton St.
Portland, OR 97202
(503) 230-7077 | www.organicclothbabydiapers.com

Baby gear, toys, rubber pacifiers, baby slings, and more. The focus is on organic, local, and sustainable goods.

OMSI SCIENCE STORE
Southeast Portland

1945 SE Water Ave.
Portland, OR 97214
(503) 797-4626 | www.omsi.edu/science-store

"Any sufficiently advanced technology is indistinguishable from magic." Arthur C. Clarke. Discover the magic of science at the OMSI Science Store. Inside you will find a thoughtfully chosen selection of science books, rocks and gemstones, telescopes, microscopes, globes, and more. They also carry a wide array of toys, maps, posters, stickers, pens, and yes, they even have astronaut ice cream!

PORTLAND FREE STORE
Southeast Portland

SE 11th & Clay St.
Portland, OR 97214

Yes, you heard right, everything in the store is free! Kind of makes the dollar store look like Park Avenue. A throwback to the flower power era, the free store collects secondhand items such as DVDs, books, clothes, shoes, and much more and "sells" them out of an old school bus. You never know what's in stock, but the price is always right. Abbie Hoffman would be proud!

ROSE CITY REPTILES
Southeast Portland

3609 SE Division St.
Portland, OR 97202
(503) 230-1361

Small pet store in Southeast Portland featuring a wide array of reptiles and amphibians. Your kids will be amazed at the sheer diversity of creatures on display here.

SHERIDAN FRUIT COMPANY
Southeast Portland

409 SE MLK Jr. Blvd.
Portland, OR 97214
(503) 236-2114 | www.sheridanfruit.com

Produce wholesaler and grocery store. Great place for a quick pit stop. Grab some of their fresh produce and a burger at their outdoor grill to go. Also a great place for bulk foods and microbrews.

STUFF
Southeast Portland

9770 SE 82nd Ave.
Portland, OR 97086
(503) 775-2056 | www.ilikestuff.com

Second hand resale store with a focus on toys.

THE LIPPMAN COMPANY
Southeast Portland

50 SE Yamhill St.
Portland, OR 97214
(503) 239-7007 | www.ippmancompany.com

Forget Party City, for over 60 years, the Lippman Co. has been Portland's go-to location for party supplies.

EVERYTHING JEWISH
Southwest Portland

6684 SW Capitol Hwy.
Portland, OR 97219
(503) 246-5437 | www.everythingjewish.biz

From Menorahs to Mezuzahs, Everything Jewish really has it all! Featuring religious and ritual items, there is also a plethora of books, CDs, toys, and games with Jewish themes. The shop also sells fine art and jewelry and Shabbat and holiday items. Everything Jewish also sells kosher meat, chicken, and Gefilte fish.

HOOPLA SPORTS CARDS
Southwest Portland

8120 SW Beaverton Hillsdale Hwy.
Portland, OR 97225
(503) 297-0285 | www.beckett.com

Vintage and modern sports trading cards for sale at this Southwest shop.

INFLATABLE KINGDOM
Southwest Portland

6830 SW Bonita Rd.
Portland, OR 97224
(503) 718-0994 | www.inflatablekingdom.com

Bouncy rooms, inflatable slides, obstacle courses, and more await your kids at Inflatable Kingdom. A great place for birthday parties and other special occasions, they also offer wonderful Summer day camps.

KAREN'S COMICS
Southwest Portland

10175 SW Barbur Blvd. #116B
Portland, OR 97219
(503) 244-0613 | www.karensbooks.com

Superheroes, Sci-Fi and more. Great little comic shop in Southwest Portland.

THE KID'S BACKYARD STORE
Southwest Portland

7400 SW Macadam Ave.
Portland, OR 97219
(503) 246-0056 | www.thekidsbackyardstore.com

If your goal is to turn your backyard into a miniature playground, then this is the place for you. Come visit the showroom and check out all the latest models.

69

GREEN FROG TOY The Pearl District

1031 NW 11th Ave.
Portland, OR 97209
(503) 222-2646 | www.greenfrogtoys.com

Large selection of unique toys, books, and games. Stop by for story time, arts and crafts, and other special events. See website for details.

HANNA ANDERSON The Pearl District

327 NW 10th Ave.
Portland, OR 97209
(503) 321-5275 | www.hannaanderson.com

Great source of children's clothing and gifts. The shop specializes in cotton clothing and offers a wide range of children's clothing made from organic cotton. There is a modest selection of children's books and toys, too.

LITTLE GREEN GROCER The Pearl District

1101 NW Northrup St.
Portland, OR 97209
(503) 297-4728 | www.littlegreengrocer.com

Family owned grocery store in the Pearl. Organic, local, and sustainable produce, cheese, groceries, wine, and beer. Plus terrific soups, salads, and sandwiches.

LITTLE URBANITES The Pearl District

916 NW 10th Ave.
Portland, OR 97209
(503) 227-8729 | www.littleurbanites.com

This hip shop in the Pearl focuses on local and sustainable baby and kids gear. One-stop shopping for kid's furniture, bedding, strollers, clothes, shoes, diaper bags, bath products, toys, books and music.

POWELL'S BOOKS The Pearl District

1005 W Burnside St.
Portland, OR 97209
(503) 228-4651 | www.powells.com

Perhaps the best bookstore in America, Powell's is Portland's crown jewel in the Pearl. They sell new and used books, with a children's section that is second to none. There are board books and chew-proof books for toddlers, while older children can peruse the aisles in search of their topics of interest. You will find rare and out-of-print titles on sports, science and nature, history, myths and legends, mystery, and science fiction. Check out the large selection of Little Golden books featuring The Lone Ranger, Little Lulu, Rin Tin Tin, Mickey Mouse, Winnie the Pooh and many more beloved characters. Visit Powell's and discover a book they will treasure forever.

VERDUN FINE CHOCOLATES   The Pearl District

421 NW 10th Ave.
Portland, OR 97209
(503) 525-9400 | www.verdunchocolates.com

Your kids will think they have entered the grand exalted vault of chocolate paradise as they walk into this elegant space. Fine chocolates at a surprisingly reasonable price. Verdun specializes in Lebanese chocolates and candy.

THE BEST DAD/CHILD
OUTDOOR PARKS & RECREATION

BIG SCREEN ON THE GREEN   Citywide

Presented by Portland Parks and Recreation, this summer cinema series is aimed squarely at families with mostly kid-friendly flicks. Films are generally shown just after dusk in various outdoor parks. Check www.portlandonline.com for details.

CONCERTS IN THE PARK   Citywide

Sponsored by Portland Parks & Recreation, Concerts in the Park is a summer series featuring the best local talent appearing at various Portland Parks. See www.portlandonline.com for details.

PORTLAND SUNDAY PARKWAYS   Citywide

Streets are closed to car traffic in five different neighborhoods, on successive weekends between May and September. Pedestrians, rollerbladers, and cyclists are free to roam a closed loop of several miles. The loops run past or through popular parks, attractions, and neighborhood events. Features live music from local bands, food from neighborhood restaurants, and a wide variety of educational and fun activities. See www.portlandonline.com for details. Neighborhood specifics are listed throughout this section.

ALBERTA PARK   Alberta

NE 22nd Ave. & Killingsworth St.

With a jogging trail, basketball court, soccer and softball fields, and a tennis court, Alberta Park is a great place for your kids to stay active all year round. Plenty of trees and green grass to frolic in, and paths to walk on.

ANKENY PLAZA   Downtown

SW Naito Pkwy & Ankeny St.

A great place to chase the pigeons. The Plaza's Skidmore Fountain, built over 120 years ago, serves a focal point for community gatherings of all stripes. Prior to the 1888 dedication, local brewer Henry Weinhard offered to pump free beer to fill the fountain! The City turned down this generous offer back then, but you can take your kids to nearby Old Town Pizza and enjoy a Henry Weinhard's Root Beer today... but be careful, the pizzeria is rumored to be haunted!

GOVERNOR TOM MCCALL WATERFRONT PARK   Downtown

Naito Pkwy between SW Harrison St & NW Glisan St.

Formerly a freeway, this park is the very embodiment of the sixties legacy: asphalt transformed into green space for the people. Named for the governor who was instrumental in its creation, this park is often referred to as Portland's backyard. In the spring, the Cherry Blossoms are spectacular as you stroll along the banks of the Willamette. Walk through the Japanese American Historical Plaza and bear witness to the Japanese-American wartime experience. In the Summer, take them to splash in the Salmon Street Springs Fountains. Walk the Eastbank Esplanade anytime of year with your kids, and watch the river flow and the boats go by. As you explore the park you will pass the Oregon Maritime Museum. Show your kids an important part of Oregon's nautical past. Take the tour aboard the sternwheeler Portland. Later, as you pass the Battleship Oregon Memorial take a moment to read the dedication plaque, and remember the brave men who served and sacrificed on that ship.

KELLER FOUNTAIN PARK   Downtown

SW Clay St. & SW 3rd Ave.

(503) 823-2223

Inspired by the many waterfalls of the Columbia River Gorge, The Ira Keller Fountain dominates this postage stamp sized park located in front of Keller Auditorium in downtown Portland. At the 1970 park unveiling, held in the wake of recent anti-war demonstrations, park designer Lawrence Halprin was quoted in The Oregonian as addressing the assembled crowd of hippies and "straights" with this advice. "As you play in this garden, please try to remember that we are all in this together." Teach your children well as you frolic in this peaceful open space.

PETTYGROVE PARK   Downtown

Between SW 1st $ SW 4th Ave. from Market to Harrison Sts.

Named for Francis W. Pettygrove, one of Portland's founders, this modest park is one of many urban oases scattered throughout the city. Green grass, tall trees, shimmering fountains, and glittering bronze statues adorn this perfect spot to take a moment to breathe and enjoy one of Portland's most charming spots for a stroll.

OUTDOOR PARKS

PIONEER COURTHOUSE SQUARE   Downtown

SW Broadway & Yamhill St.

(503) 223-1613

Often referred to as Portland's "living room" Pioneer Courthouse Square is one of Portland's most important public spaces. Formerly a school, a hotel, and a parking lot, the city acquired the space in 1979 and the park was dedicated in 1984. Located across the street from Pioneer Courthouse, the space is dominated by a red brick courtyard, and surrounding steps form an amphitheater for public events and speakers including such luminaries as the Dalai Lama.

PORTLAND FIREFIGHTERS' PARK   Downtown

SW 19th & Burnside

This park features a fountain that honors Fire Chief David Campbell, who died in the line of duty in 1911. The park also has a series of plaques that honor all of Portland's fallen firefighters, and is a great place to teach kids about the sacrifices of these brave men and women.

SOUTH PARK BLOCKS   Downtown

SW Park Ave. from Salmon St. to Jackson St.

Twelve blocks in downtown featuring two massive statues of Theodore Roosevelt and Abraham Lincoln along with myriad other works of art. The New York Times described the park as being at the "heart of the city's cultural life." Chase the pigeons with your toddlers or teach them about Presidents Lincoln and Roosevelt.

WILLAMETTE PARK   Downtown

SW Macadam & Nevada Sts.

Plenty of play structures, teeter totters, monkey bars, slides and the like for the kiddies. Wide, well-paved paths, perfect for walking or biking, and an off-leash area for dogs make this park ideal for the whole family. There is even a small beach area on the banks of the Willamette.

COLONEL SUMMERS PARK   Hawthorne/Belmont

SE 17th Ave. & Taylor St.

Formerly Belmont Park, this Southeast gem, was renamed for Colonel Owen Summers, commanding officer of the Second Oregon Volunteers Regiment in the Spanish-American War and member of the Oregon Legislature.

COMMUNITY MUSIC CENTER   Hawthorne/Belmont

3350 SE Francis St.

Portland, OR 97202

(503) 823-3177 | www.communitymusiccenter.org

Offering music lessons and presenting concerts, the non-profit Community Music Center (CMC) has worked in partnership with Portland Parks and Recreation since 1955. Offering affordable music classes and lessons to all ages, low cost music workshops, and instrument rentals, the CMC is a vital Portland asset. Check out the website for details and class schedules.

GRANT PARK   Hollywood

NE 33rd Ave. & U. S. Grant Place

Named in honor of our eighteenth president, Grant Park is also famous as the setting of local author Beverly Cleary's "Klickitat Street" books. Your kids will want to visit the Beverly Cleary Sculpture Garden for Children, which is inhabited by life-size sculptures of Ramona Quimby, Henry Huggins, and his dog, Ribsy. Afterward, take a quick drive over to Klickitat Street and take a stroll with your kids down the street where Ramona grew up! When you're finished, pay a visit to the Hollywood Library and check out the stone wall map in the children's section. Depicting the Klickitat neighborhood where Beverly Cleary grew up, stonemasons have etched key locales in both Cleary's life and in the world of her books in stone.

IRVING PARK   Irvington/Lloyd District

NE 7th Ave. & Fremont St.

With playgrounds, a fountain to splash in, an off-leash area for the four-legged children, picnic tables, and so much more, Irving Park has something for everyone.

LAURELHURST DANCE STUDIO   Laurelhurst

3756 SE Oak St.
Portland, OR 97214
(503) 823-4101

Providing year-round dance classes for children and adults. Ballet, tap, jazz, and hip-hop are offered with Pilates and ballroom dance also offered for adults. Children are taught in a circa 1914 Tudor theater-style building.

LAURELHURST PARK   Laurelhurst

SE 39th Ave. & Stark St.

Take a stroll, or feed the ducks at the duck pond. Soccer fields, tennis and basketball courts will help your kids stay active all Summer long. Swings, monkey bars, and teeter totters abound, as do miles of walking and biking paths.

MT. TABOR PARK   Mt. Tabor

Spreading out across two hundred acres, Mount Tabor Park is dominated by an extinct volcanic cinder cone rising 630 feet above the surrounding terrain. Mt. tabor also has one of the nicest playgrounds in the city, with an idyllic setting, located high above downtown, among tall conifers. Mt. Tabor is host to concerts and children's plays in the Summer. Other events include the Mt. Tabor Doggie Challenge in July and the Mount Tabor Adult Soapbox Derby in August.

OUTDOOR PARKS

OUTDOOR PARKS

CATHEDRAL PARK
North Portland

N Edison St. & Pittsburg Ave.

Named for the cathedral-like columns of the St. Johns Bridge, which bisects the park, Cathedral offers a serenity all its own. If adventure on the high seas is more your style, your lil' buccaneers will shiver their timbers while at the annual Portland Pirate Festival in September.

DAWSON PARK
North Portland

N Stanton St. & Williams Ave.

Dawson Park has a playground, basketball and volleyball courts, as well as a stage, picnic tables, and plenty of paved paths. Volunteer with your kids to feed the hungry Wednesdays at 5:30 PM with Food Not Bombs.

GEORGE PARK
North Portland

N Burr & Fessenden St.

Named for Melvin Clark George, U.S. Congressman and Portland Lawyer, this park includes a playground, walking paths, and picnic table.

KENTON PARK
North Portland

8417 N Brandon Ave.

Kenton features a playground and picnic area, plus basketball courts and ball fields.

NORTH PORTLAND SUNDAY PARKWAYS
North Portland

**Annually in June. Check out www.portlandonline.com for 2011 dates.
A 7.5 mile loop through North Portland. Traffic is closed to cars. Parks included are Kenton, Arbor Lodge, and Peninsula Parks. Local food vendors, entertainment from local bands, and too many activities and events to list in the parks and on the route!**

PENINSULA PARK & ROSE GARDEN
North Portland

700 N Rosa Parks Way

Acquired by the City in 1909, Peninsula Park retains many of the original elements and structures dating to the park's inception. Portland's nickname, the "City of Roses," is derived from the popularity of Portland's official rose, the Madame Caroline Testout, first cultivated here a century ago. There is a great playground here as well as an abundance of picnic tables, grass, and walking paths.

UNIVERSITY PARK COMMUNITY CENTER

North Portland

9009 N Foss Ave.
(503) 823-3631

Offering classes and activities for young and old alike, the center also features amenities such as a basketball court, a rock climbing wall, a gymnasium, and a computer lab.

ARGAY PARK

Northeast Portland

NE 141st Ave. & Failing St.

Conveniently located near the airport, Argay Park would make a great unwinding spot after a long flight. There is a playground, picnic tables and grills for barbecues, a basketball court, plus a baseball and soccer field.

FERNHILL PARK

Northeast Portland

NE 37th Ave. & Ainsworth St.

Fernhill features plenty of open space to roam, a shiny new play structure, baseball, softball, and soccer fields, a horseshoe pit, tennis and volleyball courts, even an off-leash area for your four legged-friends. With so much to do, don't forget the provisions. Remember to stop by the Sub Shop at 4331 NE Killingsworth for some tasty sandwiches to enjoy at Fernhill Park's picnic area.

GLENHAVEN PARK

Northeast Portland

NE 82nd Ave. & Siskiyou St.

Primarily a skate park, but also features a sports field that can be used for baseball, softball, and soccer. To reserve a sports field, call 503.823.2525. Glenhaven also has a playground, picnic tables and tennis courts. When unoccupied, tennis courts are a great place for toddlers to practice there walking and running.

JOSEPH WOOD HILL PARK   Northeast Portland

NE Rocky Butte Rd.

Former site of the Hill Military Academy, this unique Portland park is named for the academy's founder Joseph Wood Hill. The most distinguishing feature of the park is Rocky Butte. An extinct cinder cone butte and part of the Boring Lava Fields, Rocky Butte rises 600 feet into the Portland sky, providing epic views of the Columbia River and the Gorge beyond. Spectacular views of Mt. Hood, Mt. St. Helens, Mt. Jefferson, and Mt. Rainier. Breathtaking views of the Rose City skyline. A great spot to sit and watch the planes taking off and landing at Portland International Airport. The butte contains many old and interesting structures including an old jail and the Academy building now a church. There is also a fortress/castle-like structure atop the butte built by the WPA during the Great Depression. Rocky Butte is a fun place to explore and climb and best in sunny weather when the views most spectacular.

MALLORY MEADOWS PARK   Northeast Portland

NE Killingsworth St. & Mallory St.

This small park, reclaimed land that was once a parking lot, now features a playground, grass and trees, and plenty of paths to stroll on. Follow the low, serpentine wall that runs through the park with your kids and check out the tiles covering the wall. They are self-portraits made by kids from the neighborhood elementary school.

COLUMBIA CHILDREN'S ARBORETUM   Northeast Portland

10040 NE 6th Ave

A community arboretum that has served local schools for years, Columbia Children's Arboretum boasts a long meadow surrounded by tall trees, wetlands, and a wide variety of wildlife, including ducks, geese, turtles, beavers, and northern river otters.

NORTHEAST SUNDAY PARKWAYS   Northeast Portland

Annually in May. Check out www.portlandonline.com for dates and schedule. The northeast loop of Sunday Parkways Northeast links Alberta, Fernhill, Wilshire, and Woodland Parks together. Educational demonstrations, fun activities, food and music for the whole family. Eat, drink, and be merry as you wander through streets completely devoid of cars.

WILSHIRE PARK   Northeast Portland

NE 33rd Ave. & Skidmore St.

Perfect for a picnic lunch and a stroll, Wilshire Park is awash in lush green grass, tall trees, paved paths, and picnic tables. There is also a playground, soccer and softball fields, even a horseshoe pit.

WOODLAWN PARK   Northeast Portland

NE 13th Ave. & Dekum St.

With a playground, basketball court, soccer and softball fields, your little ones will have plenty to do at this charming NE Portland park. Take a little shore leave and catch "Trek in the Park" in the summer. Where else but Portland could you expect to see a live theater production of classic episodes from the original Star Trek television series? Set your phasers for fun! "The more complex the mind, the greater the need for the simplicity of play." Captain James T. Kirk, from the Star Trek episode "Shore Leave."

COUCH PARK   Northwest

NW 19th Ave. & Glisan St.

Named for Captain John Heard Couch, sea captain of great renown and one of Portland's founders, this pint-sized park packs plenty of punch with a playground, a basketball court, an off-leash area for dogs, plus lots of walking paths.

FOREST PARK   Northwest

NW 29th Ave. & Upshur St. to Newberry Rd.

Over 5,000 acres of forest, some of it old growth, spanning over 8 miles, all in a city park! Home to nearly 200 species of birds and mammals, the park's rich biodiversity makes it a treasure beyond measure.

HILLSIDE PARK   Northwest

653 NW Culpepper Terrace

With amenities such as a basketball court, soccer field, and tennis court, plus a terrific playground, there are plenty of ways to run and play at this Northwest Portland Park. The Hillside Community center at the same location features a reservable party room, rock climbing wall, and loads of activities.

NORTH PARK BLOCKS   Northwest

NW Park Ave. from Ankeny St. to Glisan St.

Portland's first supervised park, the playground opened in 1908 and was replaced in 1993 with a new playground. Bronze sculptures in the park based on Chinese mythology include a baby Elephant standing atop his Father's back. The image is meant to symbolize safe and prosperous offspring. A word of warning to dads, this statue may lead to requests for multiple piggyback rides! Afterwards head over to Deschutes Brewery Public House to refresh yourself.

SUNDAYS IN THE PARK NORTHWEST   Northwest

Annually in September. Check out www.portlandonline.com for 2011 dates. Two walking loops closed to automobiles, the first of which is the Northwest Loop. This circuit includes Couch and Wallace Parks, and the Pearl District. The second loop, the Stark & Couch Loop, is a one way loop on SW Stark & Couch. Live local music and plenty of food vendors from the neighborhood make for fun along the way. Check out the Family Center on NW 19th & Raleigh for kid's bike obstacle courses and other events. Explore the Pearl District Arts Walk, and stop at Couch and Wallace Parks for many special events.

OUTDOOR PARKS

OUTDOOR PARKS

WALLACE PARK   Northwest

NW 25th Ave. & Raleigh St.

This Goldilocks sized park is a great break after shopping on NW 23rd. See if you and the gang can locate all eleven of the mysterious bronze objects hidden in curious locales around the park. The game is afoot!

LAN SU CHINESE GARDEN   Old Town/Chinatown

NW 3rd & Everett
Portland, OR 97209
(503) 228-8131 | www.portlandchinesegarden.org

Over 400 species of plants, some over 100 years old combine to form a space like no other in Portland. Occupying an entire city block, this classical Chinese garden provides a respite from the hectic pace of city life. Gaze at beautiful Lake Zither or share a relaxing cup of tea with your children in the Tower of Cosmic Reflections.

POWERS MARINE PARK   Sellwood/Westmoreland

SW Macadam Ave. south of Sellwood Bridge

American beaver, northern river otter, numerous waterfowl, native salmon, steelhead, and lamprey all call this place home. Explore the banks of the Willamette River and discover the wild heart of the city.

SELLWOOD PARK   Sellwood/Westmoreland

SE 7th Ave. & Miller St.

This SE park boasts a 100-year-old swimming pool featuring two slides, a play structure, and spray features. Check out Sundae in the Park, a thirty year tradition, still going strong. In Upper Sellwood Park visitors will find activities such as face painting, dancers, live music, climbing wall, story time, movie in the park, ice cream and treats.

SELLWOOD   Sellwood/Westmoreland
RIVERFRONT PARK

SE Spokane St. & Oaks Pkwy

Green grass to play on, a cool beach and waterfront to explore, a boat dock, plus Monday night concerts in the Summer, and plenty of paths to take a family stroll on.

WESTMORELAND PARK   Sellwood/Westmoreland

SE McLoughlin Blvd & Bybee Blvd

With baseball, soccer, and football fields, basketball courts, tennis courts and a casting pond, your kids will have plenty of activities to choose from.

BERKELEY PARK
Southeast Portland

SE 39th Ave. & Bybee Blvd

Over sixty years ago, neighbors banded together to keep this land from being developed and Berkeley park is their legacy. Enjoy the playground area and picnic tables with your children and then run and play with them in this scenic Portland park.

EAST PORTLAND SUNDAY PARKWAYS
Southeast Portland

Annually in July. Check out www.portlandonline.com for exact dates.
A nearly five mile loop connecting Ed Benedict, Bloomington, and Lents Parks. Loads of food, fun, music, and more as you make your way through the streets that are only open to pedestrians, rollerbladers, and bikes.

HARNEY PARK
Southeast Portland

SE 67th Ave. & Harney St.

Named for General William S. Harney, whom the Sioux posthumously named "Man-who-always-kept-his-word." This park has a playground and walking paths and is a great spot for a picnic lunch. Bring a basketball and shoot some hoops with the little guys.

SEAWALLCREST PARK
Southeast Portland

SE 31st Ave. & Market St.

Seawallcrest Park features a super fun playground with a wild and wooly corkscrew slide, plus swings, teeter-totters, and a merry-go-round!

SUNDAY PARKWAYS SOUTHEAST PORTLAND
Southeast Portland

Annually in mid-August. Check out www.portlandonline for 2011 dates.
A six-mile walking loop through Southeast Portland, with streets closed to car traffic. Loop includes Laurelhurst, Sunnyside, and Colonel Summers Parks. Live music, great food, and fun events and activities for the whole family.

WOODSTOCK PARK
Southeast Portland

SE 47th Ave. & Steele St.

Plenty of space for kids to run and stretch, with a great playground. Afterward, take the rugrats to the nearby Laughing Planet Café at 4110 SE Woodstock Boulevard for a burrito or quesadilla. Wash it down with one of their amazing fruit juice smoothies.

BURLINGAME PARK
Southwest Portland

SW 12th Ave. & Falcon St.

This park has a playground for the kids, walking trails, and picnic tables. Bring a picnic lunch to enjoy after some playtime or a leisurely stroll.

OUTDOOR PARKS

GEORGE HIMES PARK
Southwest Portland

SW Terwilliger Blvd & Slavin Rd.

Named for George Himes, publisher and co-founder of the Oregon Historical Scociety, as well as its first curator. Over thirty acres of Oregon forest, laced with hiking trails that meander through the park to form one vast loop. About the only amenities available in this primal region are some picnic tables, but that's really all you'll need. Enjoy the serenity provided by this island of wilderness in the City of Roses.

HERITAGE TREE PARK
Southwest Portland

SW Corbett Ave. & Lane St.

This postage stamp-sized park totals up to less than a single acre, but it contains the historic Corbett Oak. Blow your kids' little minds as they gaze at a 300-plus-year-old tree.

HOYT ARBORETUM
Southwest Portland

4000 SW Fairview Blvd.

Home to nearly ten thousand tree species, you and your kids will marvel as you hike the extensive trail network of this urban forest.

MARQUAM NATURE PARK
Southwest Portland

SW Marquam St. & Sam Jackson Park Rd.

Nearly two hundred acres of forest thick with native hemlock, cedar, and maple trees, the park features a trail that runs from the Terwilliger Trailhead up to Council Crest. The hike is just under six miles and rises about a thousand feet to the highest point in Portland, providing spectacular views of the skyline.

PORTLAND JAPANESE GARDENS
Southwest Portland

611 SW Kingston Ave.

An authentic Japanese Garden in the city! Your children will think they have entered an enchanted realm as they explore the hushed silence and epic vistas the gardens provide.

ROSE GARDEN CHILDREN'S PARK
Southwest Portland

SW Kingston Ave.

One of the best children's playgrounds in the city. The Rose Garden Children's park features the last existing structure from the old location of the Oregon Zoo. The Elephant House picnic shelter was once the home to Rosy the Elephant, Oregon's very first elephant.

TRYON CREEK STATE NATURAL AREA
Southwest Portland

11321 SW Terwilliger Blvd.

A 645 acre state park, Tryon Creek is one of the best places in Portland for a nature hike, a bike ride or a horseback ride. Miles of trails twist and wend their way through the park. The Nature Center features a great play area for toddlers, who may find a long hike too daunting.

WASHINGTON PARK
Southwest Portland

Head of SW Park Place

Containing the Oregon Zoo, Portland Japanese Garden, Hoyt Arboretum, and the Portland Children's Museum, Washington Park is a must for Portland dads. Take the kids for a ride on the Washington Park and Zoo Railway, and see all the park has to offer. Don't miss the World Forestry Center Discovery Museum, where your kids can learn about Pacific Northwest Forests, as well as trees from around the globe.

INTERNATIONAL ROSE TEST GARDEN
Southwest Portland

400 SW Kingston Ave.

With 6,800 rose bushes and nearly 600 varieties of roses, young children will delight in the sheer beauty of this Portland treasure.

WOODS MEMORIAL NATURAL AREA
Southwest Portland

SW 45th Ave. & Woods St.

Also known as Woods Park, this scenic area offers 32 acres of woodlands and streams that are home to deer, coyotes, and great horned owls. As you walk along trails, bridges, and boardwalks, look for native trees such as douglas-fir, western hemlock, and western-red cedar.

JAMISON SQUARE
The Pearl District

810 NW 11th Ave.

An urban tidal pool in a park? The ebb and flow of the park's fountain creates a small pond of treated water that serves as the local children's wading pool. There is close access to the Portland Streetcar, too. A neighborhood favorite on a sunny day.

TANNER SPRINGS PARK
The Pearl District

NW 10th Ave. & Marshall St.

This Northwest Portland Park was formerly wetlands, with the spring fed Tanner Creek flowing into Couch Lake, which in turn flowed into the Willamette River. As the city grew and land became scarce, the wetlands and lake were filled in order to accommodate the needs of industry. Tanner Creek itself is named for the tannery built on its banks in the 1860s. In the 1990s things came full circle as a need for open space in the city became evident. The current park sits above what was once Couch Lake. Walking paths, green grass, and art make this park a welcome respite from the city streets. Sneak in a quick history lesson too. Your kids will be fascinated to know they are running and playing about twenty feet above what was once the surface of a lake.

THE BEST DAD/CHILD
SPORTS &
SPORTING EVENTS

SPORTING EVENTS

GLOWING GREENS   Downtown

509 SW Taylor St.
Portland, OR 97204
(503) 222-5554 | www.glowinggreens.com

A blacklight indoor 3D miniature golf course with a pirate theme? Ye heard right! Drag yer scurvy bones on down to the Glowing Greens in downtown Portland for the best time ye can have on dry land. A glowing, neon, blacklighted, psychedelic undersea realm awaits you as you enter the course. 3-D glasses add to the magic of the experience, and motion tripped animatronics provide heightened realism as you and yer pups explore this epic pirate experience. Afterwards take a break in their new café. Don't miss out or you just might end up in Davy Jones' locker!

NIKE TOWN   Downtown

930 SW 6th Ave.
Portland, OR 97204
(503) 221-6453 | www.nike.com

A Nike museum and retail store in close proximity to Nike headquarters in nearby Beaverton, Oregon. Explore the history of a global running shoe empire, and buy some snazzy new sneaks for the kids, delivered to you via pneumatic tube!

PGE PARK   Downtown

1844 SW Morrison St.
Portland, OR 97205
(503) 553-5400 | www.pgepark.com

Home to the Portland Timbers Major League Soccer Team. With seating for just under 20,000 for sporting events and 23,000 for concerts, PGE Park has been a Portland institution for over eighty years. Catch all the excitement of Portland State Viking Football at PGE in the fall.

HOLLYWOOD BOWL   Hollywood

4030 NE Halsey St.
Portland, OR 97232
(503) 288-9237 | www.hollywoodbowlpdx.com

Don't go all Hollywood on us after you take the kids to the Hollywood Bowl! For birthday parties, or just a night out on the town, Hollywood Bowl is the place to see and be seen. The Restaurant is much more than what you would expect at a bowling alley, with plenty of options for everybody.

OWENS SPORTS COMPLEX DELTA PARK

North Portland

10737 N Union Ct.
Portland, OR
(503) 823-1656

Featuring seven softball fields, nine soccer fields, a stadium, and a concessions building.

ROSE GARDEN ARENA

North Portland

One Center Court
Portland, OR 97227
(503) 797-9619 | www.rosequarter.com

Home to the Portland Trailblazers basketball team, this NBA franchise is Portland's lone major league team. Portlanders are justifiably proud of their Blazers, who have a long and storied history. Take your kids out for a night of basketball they won't soon forget.

MEMORIAL COLISEUM

North Portland

300 N Winning Way
Portland, OR 97227
(503) 235-8771 | www.rosequarter.com

Home to the Portland Winterhawks, a major junior ice hockey team. Ice Hockey is a great way to spend an afternoon or evening with the kids.

ERV LIND STADIUM NORMANDALE PARK

Northeast Portland

NE 57th & Hassalo St.
Portland, OR 97213
(503) 823-2525
This softball stadium named after the late legendary local softball coach is a great place to play catch or shag flies with your kids, or take a picnic and watch the adults play on the weekend.

PORTLAND ROCK GYM

Northeast Portland

21 NE 12th Ave.
Portland, OR 97232
(503) 232-8310 | www.portlandrockgym.com

Climbing is a great physical and mental challenge that is much safer than it sounds when you're learning in the trustworthy hands of the rock geeks at the Portland Rock Gym. That goes for you too, WonderDad! Take an introductory climbing class with your little one and they'll be thrilled to get up that wall before you!

SCKAVONE STADIUM WESTMORELAND PARK

Southeast

SE McLoughlin Blvd & Nehalem St.
Portland, OR 97202
(503) 823-2525

Features a popular baseball field and stadium, named after Nick Sckavone, the Portlander who helped raise the money to build the original field in 1939.

WALKER STADIUM-LENTS PARK

Southeast

SE 92nd Ave & Holgate Blvd
Portland, OR 97204
(503) 823-2525

Another of Portland's sparkling municipal softball/baseball stadiums. A great place to catch a local softball game or tourney, or if your kid is a real Bambino, to reserve for a birthday party or other special event where the kids can run wild.

BATTING A THOUSAND

Southeast

8829 SE Stark St.
Portland, OR 97216
(503) 257-2255

Great place to sharpen your skills and have a ball with your kids! Test your mettle at the batting cages and teach your kids the how to really knock it out of the park. There's also an indoor pitching tunnel, as well as video games.

WORLD LITTLE LEAGUE SOFTBALL WORLD SERIES ALPENROSE STADIUM

Southwest

6149 SW Shattuck Rd.
Portland, OR 97221
(503) 244-1133

Annually, on the second weekend of August at Alpenrose Stadium, this event charms parents and kids alike with the softball version of the national pastime at its purest. For over fifty years kids have been playing baseball at this beautiful stadium on the outskirts of Portland, and for over a decade they have been competing in the World Little League Softball World Series. Come on out to the bucolic Southwest Hills of Portland to watch these little sluggers duke it out for total World Series domination.

COOPER SPUR SKI AREA

Beyond Portland

11000 Cloud Cap Rd.
Mt. Hood Parkdale, OR 97041
(541) 352-7803

With an average annual snowfall of over 100 inches, and small crowds, Cooper Spur provides an old fashioned family ski experience between the months of November and April. The Spur's one double chairlift and ten runs are all you need for the little ones, and there is an abundance of beginner and intermediate terrain to choose from.

MOUNT HOOD MEADOWS SKI RESORT

Beyond Portland

P.O. Box 470
Mt. Hood, OR 97041
(503) 337-2222 | www.skihood.com

Located just over an hour from downtown Portland, Mount Hood is Oregon's crown jewel, and located on the flanks of this volcanic peak is Mount Hood Meadows, one of the state's largest ski resorts. With a stellar kid ski program designed to teach your kids how to schuss with the best of them, an average annual snowfall clocking in at 35 feet, and a wide range of terrain suitable for all ages and ability levels, Mt. Hood Meadows is Oregon's premier family ski destination.

OREGON STATE UNIVERSITY

Beyond Portland

Corvallis, OR 97331
(541) 737-1000 | www.oregonstate.edu

Beaver Nation unite! Come on down to Corvallis and watch the Beavers valiantly battle the opposition. Treat your kids to an action-packed thrill-fest on a bracing fall day. Warm up with some steaming hot chocolate during half-time. Go Beavs!

TIMBERLINE LODGE AND SKI RESORT

Beyond Portland

Ski & Ride School
Timberline Lodge, OR 97208
(503) 222-2211 | www.timberlinelodge.com

The only ski resort in North America featuring year round lift-serviced skiing and snowboarding. Between May and September come ski or ride on the Palmer Glacier, an epic river of snow and ice located on the south face of Mount Hood, and a remnant of the last ice age. During the deep snows of the long winter season, which average forty-five feet a year, enjoy all thirty-five runs and eight lifts available at Timberline Ski Resort.

91

UNIVERSITY OF OREGON

Beyond Portland

2727 Leo Harris Pkwy
Eugene, OR 97401
(541) 346-4481 | www.goducks.com

The fightin' Ducks are ready for whatever their opponent can throw at them, as you and your kids cheer on the University of Oregon. Kids will delight at the hijinks of the team's mascot, none other than Donald Duck himself! Go Ducks!

VALLEY LANES

Beyond Portland

9300 SW Beaverton-Hillsdale Hwy.
Beaverton, OR 97005
(503) 292-3523 | www.valleylanes.com

Get your bowl on at one the Portland area's premier bowling alleys. Family fun abounds at the Valley, with Family Night on Tuesdays and Thursdays from May to September. Take advantage of the great deals on games and food, the Pizza Scmizza pizza, and the delicious local microbrews.

THE BEST DAD/CHILD
UNIQUE ADVENTURES

APE CAVES

Just South of Mt. St. Helens, WA

You won't find any apes here, but you will find the longest lava tube in the United States. A great hiking spot jam-packed with spectacular scenery and views, the tube itself is just over 13,000 feet long. Bring a picnic lunch and a canteen, and explore the cave with your lil' spelunkers.

AROUND THE CAMPFIRE AT OXBOW: FIDDLIN' IN THE PARK

3010 SE Oxbow Pkwy.
Gresham, OR 97080

Hosted by Metro, come out to Oxbow Regional Park during Summer for music and storytelling. Friday nights feature musicians playing old-timey music on the mandolin, fiddle, and banjo. Bring your pipes to the sing-alongs. Saturday nights feature story-telling.

BONNEVILLE DAM

Cascade Locks, OR 97014

Forty miles east of Portland lies the mighty Bonneville Dam. Spanning the width of the Columbia River, this massive structure has been providing the region with electricity since the thirties. See the visitor's center, watch the fish swim past the viewing windows, or take the guided tour to really get a sense of the history and engineering behind the dam. Finish your day with a visit to their fantastic Discover Your Northwest bookstore and gift shop.

CAMPING AT OSWALD WEST STATE PARK

U.S. 101, 10 miles south of Cannon Beach
(800) 551-6949 | www.oregonstateparks.org

Campsites at Oswald State Park are located among old growth stands of Sitka Spruce one third of a mile from the beach. Wheelbarrows are provided by the Oregon Parks and Recreation Department to transport supplies from the parking lot to the campsites.

CITY OF ROSES DELTA PARK POWWOW AND ENCAMPMENT

East Delta Park
N Whitaker Rd & Union Ct
Portland, OR 97217
(503) 380-6595 | www.bowandarrowcc.org

Celebrate with Indians from across the United States at the Delta Park Powwow. Watch the dance and drum competitions, sample Native American cuisine, and check out the handcrafted art in the vendor's area.

COLUMBIA GORGE DISCOVERY CENTER & WASCO HISTORICAL MUSEUM

5000 Discovery Dr.
The Dalles, OR 97058
(541) 296-8600 | www.gorgediscovery.org

Discover the rich history of the Columbia River Gorge in a museum almost as epic as the Gorge itself. Walk through the grand entranceway to the Center and take a moment to look down. The floor beneath your feet contains a gorgeous, meandering depiction of the Columbia River flowing through it. Enter the museum proper and be amazed at the rich pageant of an area that has been continuously inhabited for over 11,000 years. Explore the geology of this dynamic region, the diversity of flora and fauna, the saga of the first peoples to call the Gorge home, and discover right along with Lewis and Clark the dawning of a new chapter in the Gorge: the coming of Westerners. Learn about the struggles of the pioneer families who traveled the Oregon Trail by covered wagon with nothing but pluck, perseverance, and faith to keep them alive. Watch the West we know today gradually evolve from the Old West, a world of rugged mountain men, grizzled prospectors, daring cowboys, and tenacious farmers. Visit the Kids Explorer Room, and check out the raptor experience. This educational program, available on weekdays, allows children to view raptors such as bald eagles up close. In addition to the easy access to hiking trails such as the Lewis and Clark and Oregon Trails the Discovery Center offers handicap accessible paved interpretive trails on the museum grounds. Explore the fascinating biodiversity of this transitional region which bridges the divide between temperate rainforest to the west and the more arid ecosystems to the east.

ENCHANTED FOREST

8462 Enchanted Way SE
Turner, OR 97392
(503) 371-4242 | www.enchantedforest.com

Enter a magical realm of Mother Goose and fairy tales come to life as you and your children wander through this truly remarkable amusement park that spreads out majestically through twenty acres of Oregon forest. For nearly forty years, kids have become immersed in a world of their imagination within the Enchanted Forest. Dads and kids begin by strolling down a path through storybook lane, wandering past houses and buildings taken directly from Mother Goose, Alice in Wonderland, Snow White, and Grimm's Fairy Tales. Step inside these structures and children become part of the narrative as they interact with animatronic versions of characters from the different stories. Enchanted Forest also features an English village, a western town, bumper cars, a kiddie train, a log plume, and much more. Enchanted Forest is a quirky antidote to sterile corporate amusement parks; a family-run business, and an Oregon one-of-a-kind. Go, and your kids will thank you for it.

97

EVERGREEN AVIATION & SPACE MUSEUM

500 Northeast Capt. Michael King Smith Way
McMinnville, OR 97128
(503) 434-4180 | www.evergreenmuseum.org

Aviation and aeronautics museum that houses the mighty Spruce Goose, designed and originally piloted by none other than Howard Hughes himself. This testament to modern engineering and one man's vision has been completely refurbished and restored from nose to tail and is waiting for you to climb aboard. Take the tour and marvel at the mind that conceived the Goose and the craftsmanship that constructed it. The aviation museum is brimming with artifacts and replicas of planes and also automobiles and tricks from yesteryear. See a full-scale replica of the Wright Brothers 1903 Flyer and you'll swear you're at Kitty Hawk with Orville and Wilbur. A brief walk takes you to the IMAX Theater where you can see movies about flight and space travel in stunning 3D. The theater is adjacent to the second exhibit hall which houses a treasure trove of NASA and military artifacts. The centerpiece of the space exhibit is a 114 foot tall Titan II Missile. The Titan II served as a launch vehicle for the Gemini and Mercury Space Capsules in the 1960's. A 30-foot pit had to be dug in the floor of the exhibit hall to accommodate this behemoth. Replicas of the Lunar Module and Lunar Rover will capture your child's imagination as will an actual X-15 Rocket Plane, an authentic Gemini Space Capsule, and real spacesuits.

MT. HOOD RAILROAD

110 Railroad Ave.
Hood River, OR 97031
(541) 386-3556 | www.mthoodrr.com

A shortline freight and passenger railroad in Hood River, Oregon. The line passes through the towns of Pine Grove, Odell, and Dee and then on to Parkdale, a mere eight miles from looming Mount Hood.

MULTNOMAH FALLS

Bridal Veil, OR
Exit 31 off I-84 East

Right off I-84 in the Gorge is a spectacular sight your kids will never forget. Multnomah Falls, cascading down over the Larch Mountain Lookout and dropping down a total of 620 feet will wow the little ones as they cross the Benson Footbridge and take in the spectacular views of both the upper and lower tiers of the falls. The cool spray of the falls is a delight, especially on a warm, sunny day.

UNIQUE ADVENTURES

OREGON COAST AQUARIUM IN NEWPORT

2820 SE Ferry Slip Rd.
Newport, OR 97365
(541) 867-3474 | www.aquarium.org

Former home of Keiko of *Free Willy* fame The Oregon Coast Aquarium is a great way to spend a day with your child or children. Visitors walk through transparent acrylic tubes surrounded by water, as sharks and other fish dart all around you. Other exhibits feature marine mammals and birds.

OREGON COUNTRY FAIR

Veneta, OR
12 miles west of Eugene on Hwy. 126
(541) 343-4298 | www.oregoncountryfair.org

Three day fair held annually the second weekend in July, in Veneta, Oregon. When it began in the Summer of 1969, The Renaissance Fair, as it was then known, was a barter and craft fair for the counter-culture. Over forty years later the Fair is one of Oregon's premier events, boasting 18 stages with entertainment including live music, comedy, theater, jugglers, stiltwalkers, fire-eaters, and other daredevils. Costumes are the norm, and leaning toward the fantastic and whimsical. The fair has stayed true to its roots, with a devotion to sustainability and individualism.

OREGON STATE FAIR

2330 17th St. NE
Salem, OR 97301
(503) 947-3247 | www.oregonstatefair.org

If your kids love a rollicking good time, plus a chance to both meet and greet your barnyard friends, then the Oregon State Fair, held late August to early September annually, is the place to do it. Since 1862, Oregonians have turned out to celebrate all that their state has to offer. Live local bands provide the soundtrack, and there are carnival rides and delicious food. The giant smoked turkey legs would make "Hagar the Horrible" proud. The fair has attractions such as the mechanical bull, pony rides, a funhouse, face-painting, kiddie rides for the younger kids and much more. There is a giant barn filled with farm animals of every kind. Watch the little piglets nurse from Momma Piggy and pet the baby goats.

RAMONA FALLS DAY HIKE

Rhododendron, OR

Seven mile loop hike accessed from the Ramona Falls trailhead. To get to the trailhead, take Hwy. 26 to Zigzag, go North four miles on the Lolo Pass Road, turn right on Rd. 1825, cross the bridge over the Sandy River, and park in the lot. The hike is not steep, but it is long, so bring water and plenty of snacks. The falls are broad and drop a hundred feet as the water cascades over the rocks and divides into myriad tiny waterfalls.

ROOSTER ROCK STATE PARK/ OMSI STAR PARTY

East of Troutdale, OR

www.rca-omsi.org

Catch the Perseid Meteor showers in August. Let the Rose City Astronomers take you on a guided tour of the night sky. Explore the Milky Way Galaxy and beyond as you watch shooting "stars" fall to Earth.

THE PUMPKIN PATCH SAUVIE ISLAND

Sauvie Island | 9-6 pm daily, open June to October.

16511 NW Gillihan Rd.

Portland, OR 97231

(503) 621-3874 | www.thepumpkinpatch.com

A veritable cornucopia of fun! Featuring a produce market, pick your own produce and flowers, a pumpkin patch, The Maize, and the spooky Haunted Maize, the Big Red Animal Barn, a café and a gift shop.

SEASIDE VOLLEYBALL TOURNAMENT

Seaside, OR

(503) 738-6391 | www.seasidebeachvolleyball.com

Watch the largest amateur beach volleyball tournament in the nation from the comfort of your living room. No it's not on TV, it's on the beach. Years ago, someone brought an old couch to watch the tournament from, and the idea caught on. Now people bring sofas, chairs, tables, and lamps, to the beach to watch the games in style. Your kids will marvel at adults engaging in pure silliness and having so much fun.

SUMMER SKIING/SNOWBOARDING TIMBERLINE

Timberline Lodge, OR 97028

(503) 272-3311 | www.timberlinelodge.com

The only ski resort open in July and August in North America is just over an hour drive from downtown Portland. Timberline ski resort offers skiing and riding to intermediate and advanced skiers only in the summer months. With epic views of the Cascades, warm sunny days and soft, forgiving snow, get here early for an adventure that is truly unique!

TILLAMOOK CHEESE TOUR

4715 Hwy. 101 N

Tillamook, OR 97141

(503) 815-1300 | www.tillamookcheese.com

Imagine Willy Wonka with cheese! Tour a century-old creamery producing some of the best cheese in America. Watch the cheese making process, sample some of Oregon's best cheese, and have some ice cream. Really, does it get any better than this?

THE PORTLAND 4T:
TRAIL, TRAM, TROLLEY, & TRAIN

A brisk walk up the Marquam Trail leads to the pinnacle of Portland, Council Crest at an elevation of 1,073 feet. Continue through the OHSU campus. Board the Portland Aerial Tram. Descend to the burgeoning South Waterfront District via the Portland Tram, and take in the expansive views of the city, Mount Hood, and Mount St. Helens through the tram's panoramic windows. Take the Portland Streetcar to 10th and Alder, then catch a MAX train at 10th and Morrison back to Canyon Road.

TURF AND SURF

With the right timing, it is possible to ski and windsurf in the same day. Timberline Lodge and Ski Resort is a mere hour and a half from downtown Portland. Timberline skis through Labor Day, and is an hour drive from Hood River, the nation's premiere windsurfing destination. One can ski or snowboard in the morning and windsurf or kayak or kiteboard in the afternoon. The possibilities are endless in a sports Mecca like this. Throw in a picnic lunch, and let em' nap in the car. Your kids will have a summer day like no other.

UFO FESTIVAL

McMenamins Hotel Oregon
310 NE Evans St.
McMinnville, OR 97128
(503) 472-8427 | www.ufofest.com

The largest UFO festival in the Pacific Northwest. Live music, authors, UFO experts, and didgeridoo making for kids.

WAHCLELLA FALLS

Bridal Veil, OR
Exit 40 off I-84 East

Located not far from Bonneville Dam, this hike is only two miles round-trip, yet it provides awe-inspiring vistas of the Gorge. The trail can be steep in spots and there are precipitous drop-offs on the side of the trail at times too, so use caution and make sure your children are safe and understand the risk. Hold their hands while hiking the steepest spots. This hike rewards richly, as you emerge from the trees and witness the falls plunging into the punchbowl below. Misty air, moss covered rocks, conifers, and the sound of rushing water all combine for an epic view, and a memory your children will treasure forever.

UNIQUE ADVENTURES

WHALE WATCHING AT NEAHKAHNIE MOUNTAIN OVERLOOK

Neahkahnie Mountain Historic Marker Turnout on Highway 101

Up to 18,000 gray whales pass through the Oregon coast on their way to the Bering Sea in Alaska from March to June. In December and January they pass through again on their way to Mexico, to breed. Neahkahnie Mountain is considered to be one of the best Whale Watching spots on the Oregon Coast. Rising 1,680 feet over the Nehalem Bay, Neahkahnie Mountain was considered home to the supreme deity by the indigenous Tillamook Indians, and is rumored to contain buried treasure!

ABOUT THE AUTHOR

Richard Geller is a freelance writer living in Portland, Oregon, with his wife and three children. He has written for *The Hood River News*, *The Rosette Gazette*, the *Jewish Review*, and *Art and Artifact*.

THANK YOUS

Rich would like to thank his wife, Leslie, whose unwavering love and support made this book possible, and his children Leo (4½), Ethan (4½), and Sela (22 months), who helped him see the City of Roses through the eyes of a child.

CPSIA information can be obtained at www.ICGtesting.com
264401BV00003B/47/P

9 781935 153610